FULL GUIDE TO BECOMING A REAL WIZARD, WITCH OR NECROMANCER

Written by Abraham Atias
Based on the Scripts of Osari the Wise

www.How-To-Become-A-Wizard.com

LIBRARY TALES PUBLISHING, INC.
244 5TH AVENUE #Q222, NEW YORK, NY, 10001
1-800-754-5016 | 1-347-394-2629
WWW.LIBRARYTALESPUBLISHING.COM

FULL GUIDE TO BECOMING A REAL WIZARD, WITCH OR NECROMANCER

Published by:
Library Tales Publishing, Inc.
244 5th Avenue, Suite Q222
New York, NY 10001
www.LibraryTalesPublishing.com

Copyright © 2011 by Abraham Atias, New york, NY.
Published by Library Tales Publishing, Inc., New York, New York
All rights to the "Scripts of Osari the Wise" are registered to Abraham Atias and the How-To-Become-A-Wizard.com corporation.

No part of this publication may be reproduced, stored in a retrieval system, or transmitted in any form or by any means, electronic, mechanical, photocopying, recording, scanning, or otherwise, except as permitted under Sections 107 or 108 of the 1976 United States Copyright Act, without the prior written permission of the Publisher.

Requests to the Publisher for permission should be addressed to the Legal Department, Library Tales Publishing, Inc., 244 5th Avenue, Suite Q222,New York, NY, 10001, 1-800-754-5016, fax 917-463-0892.

Trademarks: Library Tales, the Library Tales Publishing logo, and related trade dress are trademarks or registered trademarks of Library Tales Publishing, Inc. and/or its affiliates in the United States and other countries, and may not be used without written permission. All other trademarks are the property of their respective owners.

For general information on our other products and services, please contact our Customer Care Department at 1-800-754-5016, or fax 917-463-0892. For technical support, please visit www.librarytalespublishing.com

Library Tales Publishing also publishes its books in a variety of electronic formats. Every content that appears in print is available in electronic books.

ISBN-13: 978-0615668796
ISBN-10: 0615668798

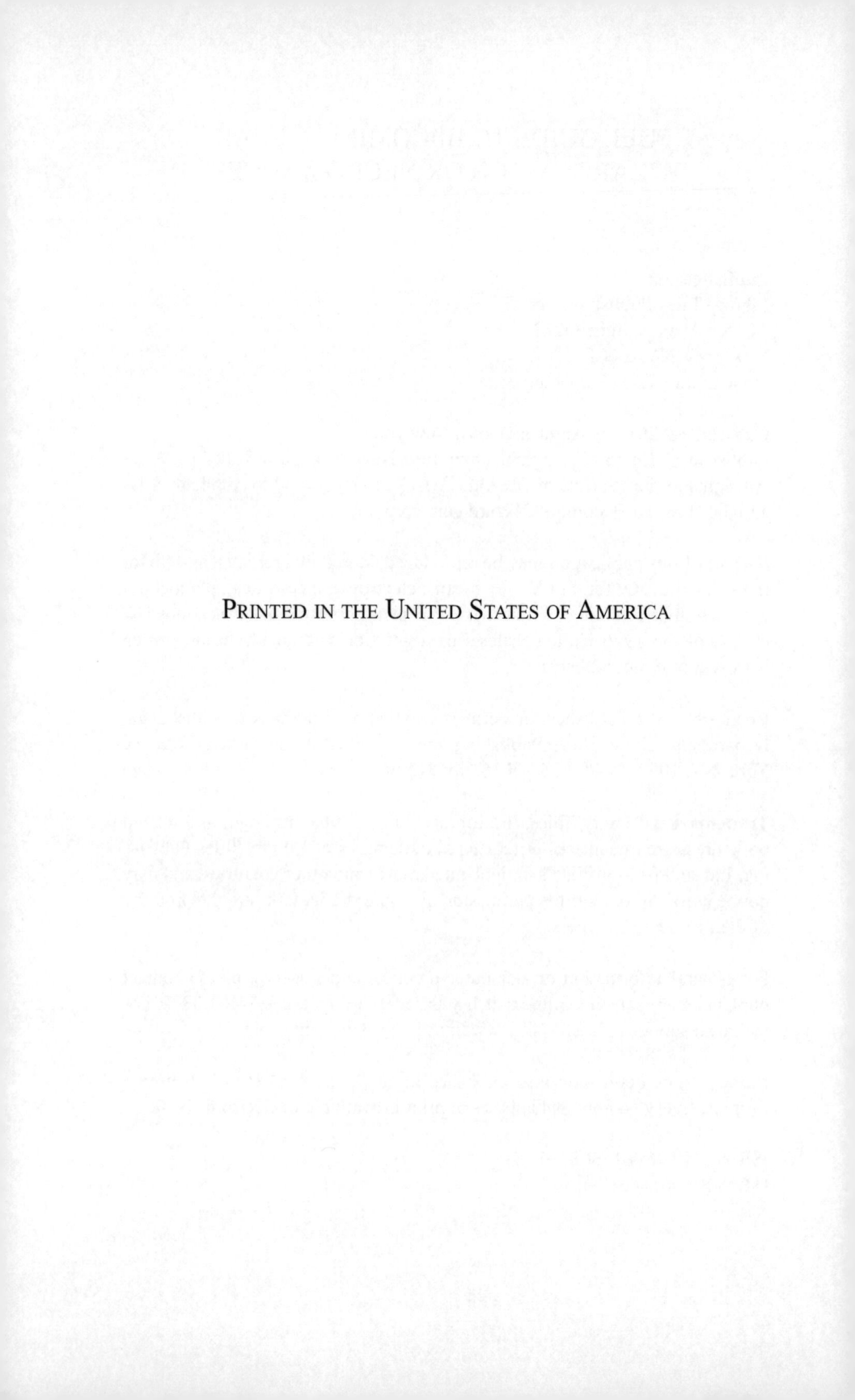

PRINTED IN THE UNITED STATES OF AMERICA

"I know... that the magic I bring to reality, starts as a thought in my mind, which is made of the same matter as God himself" - Osari the Wise, 1895.

"All that you need is just to be silent and listen to existence. There is no need of any religion, there is no need of any God, there is no need of any priesthood, there is no need of any organization" - Osho, 1989.

"Magic is the Highest, most Absolute, and most Divine Knowledge of Natural Philosophy, advanced in its works and wonderful operations by a right understanding of the inward and occult virtue of things; so that true Agents being applied to proper Patients, strange and admirable effects will thereby be produced. Whence magicians are profound and diligent searchers into Nature; they, because of their skill, know how to anticipate an effect, which to the vulgar shall seem to be a miracle." - King Solomon

Acknowledgments

We would like to express our gratitude to Danielle J Cohen for her visionary mind and her supernatural "know-how", Andrew Monroe and Tiffany Edmonds for editing and copywriting, the long list of amazing professors who granted us access to this information. We like to thank the New York Public Library and Jerry Edwards for his discoveries, in addition – we would like to thank Osari the Wise, Abraham Atias and his lasting kindred, who permitted us to review their incredible <u>Scripts of Osari the Wise.</u>

Before You Begin

Greetings, and welcome to the leading step-by-step Guide to Becoming a Real Wizard, Witch or Necromancer. In this volume, you will uncover the ancient steps to magical transformation; there are many distinctive types of magic, and this book covers the basics and beyond. Furthermore, upon reading this book you will develop a methodical plan to transform your way of life and begin practicing the magic of your choice.

The process of becoming a wizard or a witch is equivalent to that of wealth building: almost anyone is able to do it, but it demands years of hard work and commitment, significant practice and many hours of study. Please, only take this journey if you are ready to make this sacrifice, otherwise you might end up defeated and discouraged, or worse—you might harm yourself and others in the process.

This book was produced after thirty-four months of careful analysis of archaic texts, many of which are included. The content of this book is founded upon the texts of Osari the Wise. You may have never heard his name before, which is the real meaning of becoming a true wizard - you seek the admiration of God, no one else. The original scripts of Osari the Wise will be published in 2013.

Living as a sorcerer, witch or necromancer is not about exciting your friends with trickery and illusions; it is about welcoming a higher goal, becoming one with the divine world and its glamour, and adopting the privilege that the wonderful universe bestowed upon you.

Many of you first took an interest in magic on account of the many stories you hear about in fictions and folk tales, books and film; figures like Gandalf from "The Lord of the Rings", "Harry Potter" and others have always fascinated mankind.

However, you must set aside anything you think you know about sorcery, as computers produce the fantasies you see in motion pictures; on the other hand, pure wizards exposed are the ones you study about in the bible.

Therefore, anything you presume you may know about magic is faulty. However, there are a number of points you must think about before undertaking on this lifelong quest:

1 - You must be starving for knowledge and wisdom, for you will spend hours reading and practicing every day.

2 - You must be open-minded. You need to believe in your abilities and overlook your theories regarding the world, religion, God or the matters of man, and their potential powers.

3 - You must know why you hope to practice sorcery, witchcraft or necromancy. Is it the quest for comprehension? Is it to reach a certain goal? Is it to learn the mysteries of the cosmos, report to God and communicate with his angels?

Whatever the reason may be, please make sure to invest the time and effort into reading and learning about the different types of magic (all shown in this book), before deciding on a specific form of magic you wish to practice.

Whether you hope to become an alchemist, white wizard, necromancer, druid, witch, shaman or black magician, this publication will guide you throughout the steps; you will dig deep into the olden days of magic, as well as discover how to release the potential wizard within you.

How to Use This Book

This book is divided into *three* parts:

1. **Learn**
2. **Think**
3. **Act**

In the "**Learn**" section, you will learn the fundamental principles of magic and wizardry. Each chapter will be comprised of articles from the unreleased book, The Scripts of Osari the Wise, which inspired the constitution of this publication.

In the "**Think**" section, you will study the steps to becoming a magician. In order to first use magic you will need to be enlightened. Your perception of the world will have to change to that of a wizard's mentality. These are vital steps; dismissing them will lead to nothing but disappointment.

In the third and last section, **"Act,"** you will research the steps you must take to practice each unique form of magic. You may want to be a sorcerer who carries out both good and evil forms of magic or a necromancer who's able perform magical healing.

One grade of magic will not dismiss the other, and the title you give yourself -Wizard, Druid, or Witch—is irrelevant. Therefore, you must decide upon the main types of magic in which you wish to be an expert on before you begin to practice advanced forms of magic.

Let us begin.

CHAPTER 1
LEARN

CHAPTER 1: INTRODUCTION

Tales of enchanters excite most children. Fictional characters like Harry Potter and Gandalf the White, who shine as a bright light in an otherwise dark and dry planet, provide amusement and a source of inspiration to us all. They inspire children to feel empowered and battle against cold-blooded and indifferent systems. These legends and magical heroes also teach children about the existence of good and evil. But as children grow, several approaches towards magic arise; the first of which are the grave, realistic mindsets who dismiss it without thought. For them, the world is logical; anything else is hogwash.

Then we have those who sense that the universe has a divine dimension with secrets our logic cannot uncover. These individuals tend to be spiritual; they live in a world of magic, psychic readings and telepathic predictions.

Lastly, we have the profoundly God-fearing people, whose worldview is that of an eminent war between two authorities in the world: good and evil. In that view, God is aided by a host of angels and saints, and the Devil is assisted by demons, wicked spirits and living servants. Their world is jeopardized by books and films like Harry Potter, due to the severity with which magic is dealt with in their Bible.

The Jewish authority, for example, takes a hostile attitude towards wizardry and witchcraft in its various writings such as:

"A sorcerer shall not be allowed to live." (Exodus 22:17)

"Do not learn the ways of the abominations of the native people. There shall not be found amongst you ... a sorcerer, soothsayer or engager of witchcraft ... or one who calls up the dead. For it is an abomination before God, and it is on account of these abominations that God is giving you their land." (Deut. 18:9-12)

Ancient Kabbalists do speak of "the Devil" but acknowledge Satan as a representative of God, challenging the sincerity of man's actions, the strength of his beliefs and his moral fiber. Although this so-called Devil seems to seduce man to do wrong, he is not inherently a wicked being.

A study of the Book of Job bears that message: God dispatches Satan to test Job's worthiness. Just as a dentist tests the strength of a tooth by probing it, the CIA tests the morality and dependability of its agents by tempting them to divulge. God tests mankind in a similar way. A test exposes the inner worthiness of a person's actions and establishes one's nature.

When designing the physical world, God produced a non-physical system of nature that serves as an intermediate layer between God and man. Since one can use this system without immediate recourse to God, it allows for a sort of free thinking. Like all other systems, this system runs on its own—independent of God. It works whether the person is a sinner or a saint, much like gravity, the laws of physics or the laws of attraction.

Osari the Wise states that generally speaking, God desires that we make use of this world. Someone who utilizes this system of nature by constantly using the occult world is not going against the will of God, as the church would say.

A person, who postulates the phenomena of nature without caring to ask about its source, can be deceived by the system into skepticism and disbelief in God. Between God and this world lies another layer, which we shall call the occult, or the quasi-spiritual. It can shift and bend the rules of nature through magic and the use of focused thought. However, this quasi-spiritual world is not the Divine. It has its own rules and laws of operation and is possibly more compelling than the physical world, but is certainly not all powerful.

When holy people and wizards use powers beyond nature, they always stress the truth that the wonders thus formed only established God's sovereignty.

It is at this point that the threat of real corruption exists. A person, who has recognized that the rules of nature unto themselves are inadequate to interpret this power, may tap into the more non-material world and come upon a compound of unworldly powers. If he comprehends that these powers were given to him by God, this becomes a true spiritual experience. However, if he unwittingly assumes them to be self-reliant of God, then he distances himself of God, turning his powers into a source for evil.

If an individual who has no comprehension of these realities experiments with witchery or wizardry, and spells out a mumble of unfamiliar words, summons dark demons, wears peculiar outfits or participates in foreign worships, it is either artificial or wicked. It is usually artificial, but in rare cases where one has tapped into these powers, it is wicked, for the person has disconnected it from the creator. King Solomon said the beginning of our Key is to fear God, adore Him, honor Him with contrition of heart, invoke Him in all matters which we wish to undertake, and to operate with very great devotion, for thus God will lead us in the right way. Therefore, when you wish to acquire the knowledge of Magical Arts and wizardry, it is necessary to have prepared yourself and become informed when it comes to your type of magic. You must go through several steps and receive God's blessing if you ever plan to use this divine plane for your benefit.

"Without the operation of which, thou canst effect nothing; but if thou observest them with diligence thou mayest easily and thoroughly arrive at the effect and end which thou desires to attain." – (Goetia – Book of Evil Spirits.)

The ancient Celtic wizards conceived that upon birth, one of God's angels sends his hand into the mother's belly and injects your heart with spirit and life; bestowing upon you a spirit as an offering from God itself. When you are born, you are born into physical existence just like any other living thing upon this earth.

What is God?

When the majority of folks think of God, they imagine a glorious being, stationed somewhere in the galaxy or in the clouds, overseeing occurrences, human thoughts and the day-to-day managements of the whole world. Mankind is inflexible in its limited views and unlikely to ever change them.

However, a few acknowledge that perhaps there is more to God and the world than what the human race can conceive. The fact of the matter is, God is you. It is an internal force; it is the light you see when you open your eyes, the air you breathe every day, the things you feel and the items you touch. It is all around you. God is, unquestionably, the Universe itself. It is the substance of which thoughts, things and the absolute is created in its purest of forms: thought! God is the entity that manifest thoughts and transform them into existence. When the bible uttered the conviction that God created planet earth in seven days, it was indicating that God "visualized" the world in seven days, It took God seven days to design it from thought.

I would emphasize that the thoughts put forward by God and the thoughts conceived in your own intellect are the same. They occupy the same space, and so, one can say that you have the undeveloped powers of God's thoughts.

You share the same mind as God. You are it, and it is you. The greatest obstacle to progress in understanding magic, however, is that no mortal being was ever instructed and taught how to use these powers. We, as humans, must uncover these authorities alone. That is why nearly all potent enchanters and occultists are old and grey. We must reach far to comprehend this knowledge, and once we do; we become conscious to the reality that all we think we know is a mere fraction of the inexhaustible intelligence offered to us by the creator in the supernatural divine. So our access to the true knowledge of magic is restricted by our understanding of it.

Studying this book and grasping the conceptions delivered in this book will aid you in acquiring a greater comprehension of how to make use of and profit from the privileges offered to us by the divine, how to use your thoughts to form magic, to charm, spell and bear non-fictitious magic to the universe, and how to use that magic to manipulate the un-manifested. I wish you a wonderful journey into the world of wizardry and witchcraft.

Magic

As an intelligent student of magical literature, I am amused by the uninformed criticism directed against Magic. Since childhood we have believed in the Bible. In a rush to become adults, and cast off childish beliefs, we are likely to rashly reject both classics as nothing more than folklore and anthropology. Though we seek and find Kabalistic knowledge hidden in the Bible, we are slow to use the Kabbalists works to reveal the Bible's mysteries.

I do not deny that "magic" exists: if it is an illusion, it is at least as real as everyday life, for it is evidence of some cause. Now, the fact of cause and effect is our starting point. What causes my illusion of seeing a spirit in the Triangle of Art? A psychologist will answer, "That cause lies in your brain." European children will reply that the Universe is the creation of the Ego, or self. English school children will say that the Universe lies in infinite Space. And Hindu children also refer to a Universe in infinite Space, but they call it Akasa. The Hindu Akasa relates to the "Third Eye," which refers again to the brain.

All sense-impressions are dependent on the brain. Therefore, illusions are sense-impressions as much as "realities," for they depend on brain changes. Magical phenomena, however, are a special sub-class of sense-impressions because they are willfully caused by the series of "real" operations of ceremonial magic. These consist of:

(1) Sight. The circle, square, triangle, vessels, lamps, robes, implements, etc.

(2) Sound. The invocations.

(3) Smell. The perfumes.

(4) Taste. The Sacraments.

(5) Touch. The circle, square, triangle, vessels, lamps, robes, implements, etc.

As an intelligent student of magical literature, I am amused by the uninformed criticism directed against Magic. Since childhood we have believed in the Bible. In a rush to become adults, and cast off childish beliefs, we are likely to rashly reject both classics as nothing more than folklore and anthropology. Though we seek and find Kabalistic knowledge hidden in the Bible, we are slow to use the Kabbalists works to reveal the Bible's mysteries.

I do not deny that "magic" exists: if it is an illusion, it is at least as real as everyday life, for it is evidence of some cause. Now, the fact of cause and effect is our starting point. What causes my illusion of seeing a spirit in the Triangle of Art? A psychologist will answer, "That cause lies in your brain." European children will reply that the Universe is the creation of the Ego, or self. English school children will say that the Universe lies in infinite Space. And Hindu children also refer to a Universe in infinite Space, but they call it Akasa. The Hindu Akasa relates to the "Third Eye," which refers again to the brain.

All sense-impressions are dependent on the brain. Therefore, illusions are sense-impressions as much as "realities," for they depend on brain changes. Magical phenomena, however, are a special sub-class of sense-impressions because they are willfully caused by the series of "real" operations of ceremonial magic. These consist of:

(1) Sight. The circle, square, triangle, vessels, lamps, robes, implements, etc.

(2) Sound. The invocations.

(3) Smell. The perfumes.

(4) Taste. The Sacraments.

(5) Touch. The circle, square, triangle, vessels, lamps, robes, implements, etc.

(6) Mind. The combination of all these and reflection on their significance.

These unusual impressions (1-5) produce unusual brain-changes; hence their mental summary (6) is also of an unusual kind. As the brain reflects on extraordinary sensory memories, these momentary reflections are extraordinary as well. Ceremonial magic generates brain changes in which the "effects" refer only to the appearance of sense-impressions to the magician. His spirit, his conversation, his possible shocks, and so on, lead him to ecstasy, or even to death or madness.

But can any of the effects described in the *Goetia* be obtained? And, if so, can you give a rational explanation of the circumstances? Yes. I will explain.

The spirits of the *Goetia* are portions of the human brain. Following the logic of Mr. Spencer's projected cube, they represent methods of stimulating or regulating particular spots through the eye. The names of God are vibrations calculated to gain increasingly complex control of the brain. The names' vibrations first establish brain functions relative to the subtle world in order to gain general control of the brain. One may then control the brain in detail by invoking a particular rank or type of the Spirit. Finally, when a particular Spirit is named, one may control a special portion of the brain.

Perfumes aid ceremonial magic through smell. Usually perfume will diffuse within a large area, but one may also associate perfumes with letters of the alphabet; doing so enables one, by a Kabalistic formula, to spell out the Spirit's name. I need not discuss these points in detail; the intelligent reader can easily fill in what is lacking. If, then, I say, with Solomon, "The Spirit Cimieries teaches logic," I refer to my own logic being stimulated and developed through 'The Invocation of Cimieries.' This statement is rational and refers to material reality, for it is independent of any objective hierarchy. Philosophy has nothing to say on this matter. Science can only suspend judgment, pending a methodical investigation of the alleged facts.

Solomon promises us that we can (1) obtain information through bringing up facts from the subconscious; (2) destroy our enemies by realizing the illusion of duality, and by exciting compassion for our opponents; (3) discern the subtle voices of nature by listening carefully, much as a child understands the differences between a cat's purr and meow; (4) obtain treasure through business acumen; (5) heal diseases of the body by strengthening the tissue's connection to the brain, and so on. I have taken these five powers at random for considerations of space forbid me to explain all.

Magic is essentially a series of small observational experiments on the body. Those who will conduct the rituals intelligently need not fear the result. I have plenty of health, treasure, and logic, but I have no time to waste. *There is a lion in the way.* These practices are useless to me, but for the benefit of others I give them to the world together with this explanation that I trust will enable many students to succeed where others who viewed the question objectively failed.

The Definition

"Magic is the Highest, most Absolute, and most Divine Knowledge of Natural Philosophy. Advanced in its works and wonderful operations by a right understanding of the inward and occult virtue of things; so that true Agents being applied to proper Patients, strange and admirable effects will thereby be produced. Whence magicians are profound and diligent searchers into Nature ; they, because of their skill, know how to anticipate an effort,* the which to the vulgar shall seem to be a miracle."

The ancient theologian **Origen** said that the Magical Art does not contain anything Evil, or subject to contempt or scorn; thus Origen distinguishes *Natural Magic* from that which is *Diabolical*.

The early Christian theologian **Apollonius Tyannaeus** exercised only *Natural Magic* by which he performed wonderful things.

Philo Hebraeus said that "true *Magic* is that which increases our understanding of the Secret Works of Nature. It is so far from being contemptible that the greatest Monarchs and Kings have studied it. Nay! No Persian was allowed to reign who was not skilled in this Great Art."

This Noble Science often runs afoul, from *Natural* it becomes *Diabolical*, and from True Philosophy comes Black Magic. Those followers who are not capable of that High and Mystical Knowledge fall into temptations of Satan, and are misled by him into the Study of the Black Art. Hence it is that all Magic is disgraced, and they who practice it are vulgarly esteemed Sorcerers.

The Soul

Osari the wise observed and uncovered that the soul (human spirit) is the infinite fraction of God. This is yet a second claim that nurtures the conviction that you and God are the same. The soul materializes from the great hall of spirits; think of it as a headquarters of sort, a glorious recycling hub for mortal spirits, an un-manifested realm, stationed deep inside the spiritual world, where all souls exist in the form of energy. Souls come into and get out of their avatars daily. And so, when a mortal is born, his soul temporarily accommodates a human body, a spiritual yet physical machine for it to live in. That machine, that body, is you.

And so you are, in fact, chartering your physical body from the earth. You only 'possess' it for a short while. You were granted a life force by God, and you are fortunate to experience it here on this earth. Imagine God, in today's terms, as a computer operating system. Administering billions of independent softwares, each software has its own purpose. When a software no longer has a purpose, it is terminated by God, the one who created it. In fact, you could make the claim that you are, also, a software program. You live inside a physical body, and you experience life (the world) from within that body. Your soul is, for that matter, the legal property of God, while your body is a mere tool with which you use to experience God's creation. You are an avatar, activated by a soul, located in the divine.

This understanding will help you enhance your command of these religious, mystical and divine notions illustrated in this book. The concepts brought forth in this book may appear to refute this theory, but take heed: we only present the facts as the accounts of magic present them. It should be your intention to study and fathom the numerous opinions and viewpoints of those who use magic, and this book will accommodate you in that respect.

The soul lives within humans and all other breathing things, including spiritless bodies and the universe as a whole. The Mayan sorcerers supported the same philosophy that objects, such as waterways and mountains, had their own intellect, their own soul.

The spirit has three elements. The Zohar, a masterwork of Jewish magic, describes them:

"Breath"
"Spirit"
"Soul"

<u>Breath (Nephesh)</u> – The breathing mortal being: it feels desire, hate, affection, grief and most importantly, can expire (die, cease to breathe). The Breath is simply an "air-breather." Animals and weeds also are a Nephesh—they breathe air. It is the origin of one's physical and mental nature. The other two parts of the spirit are slowly designed over time; their growth relies on the behavior and faith of the body and the mind. They only fully endure in humans awakened spiritually.

<u>Spirit (Ruah)</u> – The midpoint soul: it consists of the ethical purities and the capacity to discriminate between good and evil. In present-day parlance, it equates to the psyche.

<u>Soul</u> – the higher intellect or super-soul: this discriminates mankind from all other life forms. It links to the intellect and allows one to hold some consciousness of the existence and presence of a supreme being. According to Osari the Wise, after death the soul travels to the glorious halls of spirits where it is submitted to recover, entering into a form of bliss. It returns to the source, where it delights in "The kiss of the beloved." Supposedly, after rebirth, soul and spirit are reunited in an eternally metamorphosed state of being. Jewish Sorcerers maintain that there are two more portions of the human soul, the "Chayyah" and the

"Yehidah." These are considered to represent the levels of self-generated awareness and to be within the control of only a few elected human beings.

Chayyah – The piece of the intellect that allows one to have a grasp of the supernatural and tap into it.

Yehidah – the highest level of the psyche, in which one can obtain complete unity with God and the divine world.

In Simple English:

The soul is a fraction of God's liveliness inside you. God sees, hears and acts through you; you are an agent of his essence here on planet earth. The greater command you have of your soul, the greater the authority of the supernatural is at your rule. In fact, it is God's desire that you attain some authority over the divine, as long as you are doing so in his name.
You and God are "produced" of the same substance. By that notion, you are God. And as long as you experience witchcraft, you must honor God and acknowledge him as the dominant source of your powers.
Only recognize that you are an embodiment of a higher being. Your soul controls that "Avatar" and it is an extraordinary design. How many people do you know who think of themselves as "Avatars of God"? Very few, which is why only a handful of wizards ever attain true power through enlightenment; they learn to converse with higher power, the source: God.

From the scripts of Osari The Wise
(section 9, page 36)

"Your intellect is the fundamental attachment between you and God; The miraculous merits which make you yourself; are the very traits of God himself; and it is your end as a wizard, witch or necromancer to use them in his name and for a just cause. From the moment of creation, you are a daydreamer; you imagine, think and never stop fantasizing, just as a child should. As you grow, your guardians force you to acknowledge "their reality"; slowly killing the wizard inside you. This trickery was invented by mystery destroyers and magic murderers, and the only way to defeat it is if we will all return to our childhood state, day dreaming and fantasizing." – (Osari the Wise;1907.)

Understanding Magic

Magic is the practice of manipulation of energy to achieve a desired result, usually by techniques described in various conceptual systems. Ideas of religion, mysticism, occultism, science, and psychology influence the practice of magic.

One must find out for oneself and make sure beyond a shadow of doubt to ask "Which, what, and why?" thus being conscious of the proper course to pursue. The next thing is to understand the conditions necessary to follow. After that, one must eliminate from oneself every element alien or hostile to success and develop those parts of oneself needed to control the previously mentioned conditions.

Magic is the procedure of manipulation of the conscious mind to attain a sought after result, usually by methods depicted in various conceptual systems. Conjectures of religion, religious mysticism, occultism, psychology and mindset impact the individual exercise of magic.

The word 'magic' is used in connection to the supernatural abilities of the Mage; Magic is a divine force that generally includes associative thinking, or the capacity of the human intellect to influence the physical world. The only science present for investigation today that can illustrate and clarify the essence of magic is known as Quantum Mechanics.

Generally connected to supernatural beliefs and conventions, magic is a medium for human beings to influence the physical world around them by means of heterogeneous charms, ceremonies or even desires, in either a destructive or a constructive way. The capacity to execute magic is generally a biological trait or an acquired technique.

However, the Wizard understands that the absolute Will of every man and every woman is already in flawless tune with the divine Will. It is the Wizard's Great Work to attempt to abolish the barriers that foil his or her perfect understanding of that Will and then carry on to execute it.

Apart from those willed feats of a mundane kind, many cases of executed magic require the use of ceremonies. Most magical ceremonies require work with heavenly spirits (Gods, demons, spirits, saints, etc.) and obtaining supernatural mental states, such as necromantic trance. There are numerous objectives for comporting a magical ritual, including:

Initiation
Banishing
Consecration
Devotion
Celebration
Evocation
Invocation

Purification
Vision seeking
Illusions
Elemental Magic (Manipulating Water, Air and Fire)
Practical purposes

There is evidence of complex techniques of magic in countless archaic cultures. The next list includes practices of magic that are fairly modern:

Chaos magic
White Magic
Enochian magic
Druidism
Goetic magic
Kabalistic Magic
Ceremonial magic
Shamanism
Witchcraft & Voudon
Necromancy

Magic is merely a term to tap into formerly neglected or unconditioned human potential. There was a time when countless individuals could execute feats that would conventionally be spoken of in the common tongue as magic, but unfortunately over the centuries, as science and reason and so-called "logical thought" came into ascendance, what had been learned slowly became unlearned. It was eventually abandoned and forgotten in the relentless pursuit of what was the equivalent of the next big fad, and the old ways faded away.

This of course, occurred for a variety of reasons. For some, it was a simple lack of practice and determination. For others, it was that they had never developed these talents in the first place. Yet for others, there was the compelling transformation from the intelligent crafts to the more socially conventional modes of science and logic, and it is only in recent times that the narrow-mindedness has settled enough to allow practitioners to, once again, be open with their art—at least in part of the western world.

As to how to comprehend it, the preliminary step is to develop self-discipline, control and determination. It is stupendous what the human being is capable of, once we understand how to focus our thoughts and polish it. However, studying and applying magic is not swift or casual, as you will see. It takes time and effort and is undoubtedly not for individuals seeking overnight results.

For those interested in learning proper techniques for focusing their will and practicing magic, I would suggest completing the steps in this book. "Study" is the beginning of all knowledge, and practice does indeed make perfect.

First, understand that there is not one set "form" of magic, and that in fact, many wizards have entirely distinctive approaches to provoking the same outcome; your way of life alters and the inquiries you perform change the energy you produce. If you focus most of your concentration on becoming a druid, you must exercise your fondness and adoration towards nature and everything in it; if you focus your energy on becoming a necromancer, then you must connect with the suffering of the dead and comprehend the authorities of demons and the lord of death.

From the scripts of Osari The Wise
(section two, page 18)

"The peaceful equilibrium between magic, logic, fairness and common practicality was intermitted by the Catholic cathedral in the early 500s; a sorcerer will fear teaching the magical lessons of his pack to his kin, from fear of criminal prosecution by the church. A mother will fear to mend or charm for fear of hanging from a gibbet as a witch, whose hour had come.

Little by little, the privileges of magic will be defeated by the overflow of human reason in ages to come, magic will be forgotten, and the good will of God will no longer be accounted for; until, one day, it shall reoccur.

For the bewilderment of the Catholics, Israelites and the Greeks, God's angels shall come down upon us with both fury and fondness, the righteous shall prosper, and the evil shall fall..." – Osari the Wise, 1907.

History of Magic

The Hellenic religions had mighty supernatural components, and in Egypt, a large number of mystical papyri. Judaism had seers, mediums and men who governed demons; these authorities contain ancient instances of the paranormal myths that later came to be part of Western cultural assumptions about the system of magic. They include primitive examples of:

- The utilization of "charming words" said to have the authority to govern spirits;

- The use of wands, Staves and other ritual tools;

- The use of a magic ring to safeguard the wizard against the spirits that he is calling upon; and the use of enigmatic symbols or sigils which are thought to be useful when soliciting spirits.

- The use of spirit mediums;

From the 13th century, the Jewish Kabbalah exerted authority on Christian occultism, giving rise to the first grimoires and the academic occultism that would develop into Renaissance magic.

The fundamental divinity of Christian demonology inspired wizards to strengthen themselves with fasting, worships and sacraments, so that by using the sacred names of God in the divine languages, they could use supernatural forces to force demons into materializing and serving their generally impure or greedy magical goals.

The seven arts distinctly forbidden by canon law, as set forth by Johannes Hartlieb in 1456—were:

1. Nigromancy
2. Geomancy
3. Hydromancy
4. Aeromancy
5. Pyromancy
6. Chiromancy
7. Scapulimancy

Both poor and rich, in the 15th and 16th centuries, showed a great fascination with these arts, which exuded an exotic charm by their ascription to Jewish, Gypsy and Egyptian sources. There was great uncertainty in distinguishing practices of magic. The intellectual and spiritual tensions erupted in the Early Modern witch craze, further reinforced by the turmoil of the Protestant Reformation, especially in Germany, England, and Scotland.

Both middle class and the elite, in the 15th and 16th centuries, exhibited a considerable captivation with these arts, which oozed out an unusual appeal by their attribution to Jewish, Gypsy and Egyptian origins. There was great bewilderment in differentiating systems of magic. In Britain, the Witchcraft Act of 1735 petitioned that individuals not be scolded for consorting with spirits, while bogus conjurors professing to be able to invoke spirits could still be fined as con artists.

Recent interest in charming took place around the end of the nineteenth century, where Symbolism and other branches of Romanticism inspired a modernized fascination with spiritualities.

The late 19th century gave rise to a few magical groups, such as the Hermetic Order of the Golden Dawn. The Golden Dawn symbolized the climax of this overwhelming interest in magic, appealing to cultural luminaries like William Butler Yeats, Arthur Machen, and Arthur Machen.

In general, the 20th century has seen an increase in open interest of different customs of supernatural practice, and the groundwork of a number of practices and forms of magic, ranging from the religious to the metaphysical.
Wicca is one of the more publicly known traditions within Neopaganism, a magical religion inspired by medieval witchcraft, with influences including the Hermetic Order of the Golden Dawn and Crowley. Ruickbie shows that Wiccans and witches define magic in many different ways and use it for a variety of purposes. Despite the diversity of opinion, he perceives the result upon the practitioner is generally a positive one. Wicca is one of the more publicly recognized customs within Neopaganism, a mystical religion inspired by archaic witchcraft, with influences including the Hermetic Order of the Golden Dawn and Crowley.

The conviction that one can manipulate divine powers by prayer, sacrifice or invocation goes back to primitive religion and is present in early records such as the pyramid scrolls and the Indian Vedas. Sigmund Freud explained that *"the associated theory of magic merely explains the paths along which magic proceeds; it does not explain its true essence, namely the misunderstanding which leads it to replace the laws of nature by psychological ones."*

Freud emphasizes that what led primitive men to come up with magic is the power of wishes:

> *"His wishes are accompanied by a motor impulse, the will, which is later destined to alter the whole face of the earth in order to satisfy his wishes. This motor impulse is, at first, employed to give a representation of the satisfying situation in such a way, that it becomes possible to experience the satisfaction by means of motor hallucinations. This kind of representation of a satisfied wish is quite comparable to children's play, which succeeds their earlier purely sensory technique of satisfaction. As time goes on, the psychological accent shifts from the motives for the magical act onto the measures acted out – that is, onto the act itself. It thus comes*

to appear as though it is the magical act itself which, owing to its similarity with the desired result, alone determines the occurrence of that result."

Therefore, we learn that magic is not simply the command of wishes; it is a system of faith sustained by mana, numen, chi, or kundalini, which exists in all living things. Sometimes this force is focused upon a magical object, such as a ring, stone, charm, or dehk, which the conjuror can manipulate, and sometimes the enlightened magician himself can generate this power by meditation only.

According to Osari the Wise, a proficient wizard manipulates his mana and has the abilities to shift and manage his mana through what is called "Magical Meditation" (see the chapter "Meditation" in this book to learn how to utilize this system of magic).

Manipulation of the earthly elements occurs by utilizing the command of the wizard and his symbols, or objects, which are representative of the elements. Some Wizards use the atmospheric forces of Earth, Air, Water, and Fire.

Manipulation of Energy is conceived to be the use of energy from the human body. It is most commonly depicted as the application of the hands, while the mouth uses a commandment of power.

Manipulation of symbols: Disciples of magical philosophy suppose that symbols are for more than mere illustration: they can assume a material trait of the occurrence or entity that they symbolize. Another outlook is that sigils, in particular, can possess magical powers. By influencing symbols, or sigils, one can influence reality, or the reality that the symbol represents.

According to the Law of Similarity, the wizard concludes that he can provoke any effect he asks for, merely by emulating it; he understands that whatever he does to a physical object will affect the individual with whom the object was once in contact, whether it constituted as a part of his body or not.

Most wizards, conjurors and witches refurbish their mana by different forms of meditation, visualization, enhancing spells, rituals and prayer.

From the scripts of Osari The Wise
(section 1, page 77)

"Magic is the oldest grade of individualistic relationship to God, The almighty draws his domestic strengths from worship and faith; when you pray, you take away from him, and when you connect to the divine, you grant him by spreading his fame among the people. Do magic in God's fame, relish the talents he bestowed upon your making and your undying energy" – Osari the Wise, 1907.

Magic, Ritual, and Religion

Many religious customs and convictions seem equal to, or very similar to, magical thinking. The link between magic and ritual is religious supplication. This generally forces a sacrifice to a mystic being or deity. The person offering the prayer generally asks God to interject on their behalf.

The contrast is that worship demands the permission of a God with an individual will, who can confute or welcome the request. Osari the Wise claim that magic, by contrast, is effective by virtue of the procedure itself and by the determination of the wizard's will; Alternatively, the wizard believes he can control the spiritual beings approached by his charms.

Why Would Magic Fail?

Generally, when worship fails, it means that the deity has chosen not to allow it; when charming fails, it is due to a fault in the casting of the charm or spell and the mental state of the individual who carries it out. Thus, magical practices tend to focus on precise formulaic correctness and are less unceremonious than prayer. Ritual is the wizard's failsafe, the key to any wish for attainment, and the rationalization for failure. A potential exception is the practice of confidence, where the discipline of faith in itself brings about a sought after result.

By achieving true "magical enlightenment", you tap into your subconscious mind and the link to the divine; hence, increasing your chances of successful charming.

Magic in Animism and Folk Religion

Some grade of shamanic connection with the spirit world appears to be practically general in the early evolvement of human societies. Much of the Babylonian and Egyptian illustrated writing appeared to originate from the same authorities.

Although native magical practices linger to this day, some colonies in the past transitioned from nomadic to rural societies, and with this change, the evolution of spiritual life reflected that of civic life. As tribal Wiseman grew into kings and governments, shamans and wizards transformed into churchmen and a priestly caste. While the shaman's duty was to confer between the tribe and the spirit world, the priest's role was to pass on guidance from the deities to the town.

This change symbolizes the first usurpation of power by detaching magic from those engaging in that magic. It is at this period of evolution when highly systematic and complicated rituals, began to surface, such as the funeral rites of the Egyptians and the sacrifice practices of the Babylonians, Aztecs and Mayans.

Magic and Monotheism

Conventional religions identify magic as outlawed witchcraft or occultism, and have often accused claimed practitioners with varying extents of severeness. Men of science were quick to reject all such manifestations as trickery and delusion; nothing more than fraudulent schemes. Some suggest that the present-day admiration of the prosperity gospel represents a return to occult thinking within Christianity.

Jewish Magic

Primitive Judaism perpetuated and enriched conventions of magic. In effect, all works claim, or ascribe to archaic authorship. For example, Sefer Raziel HaMalakh, an Astro-magical source partially grounded on a mystical guidebook of ancient times, Sefer ha-Razim, was handed to Adam by the deity Raziel after being expelled from Eden.

Another celebrated work, the Sefer Yetzirah, reputedly dates back to the father Abraham. These claims are rooted in Apocalyptic texts, which affirms that cryptic proficiency such as the use of magic, prophecy and astrology, was passed on to mankind in the olden days by the two deities, Aza and Azaz'el, who escaped from heaven (see Genesis 6:4).

Christian Magic

Looked upon with great skepticism by Christianity from the time of the Church elders, it was, however, never quite cleared whether magic is permitted. It involved ancient relics or holy water in comparison to "godless" necromancy, incorporating the appeal to demons—Goetia. The contrast became explicitly contentious during the primitive witch-hunts, with some sources, condemning all magical conventions as impious, while others depicted white magic as holy.

The current Catechism of the Catholic Church debates divination and magic under the title of the First Commandment. It is prudent to authorize the probability of divinely gifted prediction, but it renounces "all other forms of divination":

(2116) reject all forms of divination, recourse to Satan or demons, conjuring the dead or other practices falsely supposed to "unveil" the future. Consulting horoscopes, astrology, palm reading, interpretation of omens and lots, the phenomena of clairvoyance, and recourse to mediums all conceal a desire for power over time, history, and, in the last analysis, other human beings, as well as a wish to conciliate hidden powers. They contradict the honor, respect, and loving fear that we owe to God alone.

The catechism expresses skepticism towards common conventions of folk Catholicism without prohibiting them clearly:

(2117) Wearing charms is a reprehensible act. Spiritism often implies divination or magical practices; the Church for her part warns the faithful against it. Recourse to so-called traditional cures does not justify either the invocation of evil powers or the exploitation of another's credulity.

Spells and Divinations

The leading model of magical convention is the spell, a ritualistic technique pre-arranged to attract a particular effect. Spells can be uttered, inscribed or physically composed using a distinct set of components. Numerous things can produce the failure of a spell, such as a negligence to obey the precise procedure, overall resources being ineffective, to a scarcity of mana (magical energy), magical ability, or the lack of determination.

Another well-known magical custom is divination, which attempts to uncover knowledge about the past, present or future. Classes of divination include Astrology, Augury, Cartomancy, Chiromancy, Dowsing, and Fortune telling, Geomancy, I Ching, Lithomancy, Omens, Scrying and Tarot reading.

Necromancy

Necromancy is a system that professes to include the evocation of, and communication with, spirits of the deceased. This is occasionally achieved merely to converse with departed loved ones; it can also be achieved to gain knowledge from the spirits, as a type of prophecy or to command the aid of those spirits in carrying out various ambitions, as part of casting a spell.

Contagious magic entails the use of physical elements that were once in physical touch with the soul or a thing, which the wizard aspires to effect. Sympathetic magic requires the use of representations or physical entities that in some way take after the individual one expects to influence; voodoo dolls are an example.

Other widespread classes given to magic include High and Low Magic, the appeal to godlike authorities or spirits respectively, with goals prominent or personal, suiting to the type of magic. Another difference is between "manifest" and "subtle" magic. Subtle magic conventionally applies to magic of fiction, slowly and occasionally reshaping the physical world, whereas manifest magic is magic that promptly occurs as a result.

The Focus of this Book

This book centers upon fundamental comprehension of general magic. This book does not inspire or deject one kind over the other; magic in itself is delightful and must be used for valid reasons. However, if you aim for a personal enmity and desire to practice fewer harmful forms of magic, it is your exclusive choice to make.

Magical Traditions

Another approach of categorizing magic is by "traditions," which in this frame of reference conventionally refer to systems of magical belief and convention correlated with different cultural groups. Some of these antediluvian conventions are highly particular and culturally confined. Others are more eclectic and syncretistic. These conventions can include both divination and spells.

Some examples of magical conventions include:

Alchemy, Animism, Asatru, Black Magic, Bön, Candomble Jeje, Ceremonial magic, Chaos magic, Druidry, Feri Tradition, Haitian Vodou, Hermetic Qabalah, Hermeticism, Hoodoo, Huna, Kabbalah, Louisiana Voodoo, Nagual, Obeah, Onmyōdō, Palo, Pow-wow, Psychonautics, Quimbanda, Reiki, Santana, Santería, Satanism, Seid, Setianism, Sex Magic, Shamanism, Shinto, Sigil Magic, Taoism, Thelema, West African Vodun, Wicca, Zos Kia Cultus, etc.

Dark Magic

Dark magic, or generally referred to as black magic, is the belief of conventions of sorcery that draws on adopted malicious authorities. This form of magic is conjured when aspiring to destroy, steal, harm, cause hardship or death, or for personal gain without respect to damaging results to others.

The term, "black magic" is generally used by those who do not support of its functions; and is frequently in a ritualistic setting. The argument of "magic is colorless" advocates the affirmation that not everything that is labeled as "dark magic" has malicious purposes behind it. Some would consider it to have favorable and well-disposed uses.

These functions would embrace the exterminating of sicknesses or evil possessions. Dark wizards who successfully make use of magic in this way claim that the outcome itself is malicious by compelling death to insects; but as an indirect outcome of black magic, good can be a result, such as in the form of fewer pests around, etc. In this school of thought, there is no detachment between good and evil magic because there is no all-embracing principles against which magic is measured.

In fiction, dark magic will quite frequently be interchangeable with evil occultism. In many common video games, white and black magic is merely used to differentiate between remedial or protective spells, such as a divine cure, and offensive or elemental spells, such as fire, respectively, and does not carry a fundamental positive or negative implication.

Black and White Magic

The contrast to dark magic is pure (white) magic. The distinctions between black magic and white magic are disputable, though many theories mostly fall within the following categories:

The "All as One" theory declares that all grades of magic are evil, without regard to color (white or black) and is ordinarily connected with Satanism. People who affirm this belief include those within the popular branches of Christianity, Islam, and Hinduism.

The "Dark Creed" notion proclaims that dark magic is the use of "forces of darkness," generally viewed from a sinister point of view. This may clash with pure magic, banking on the practitioner's recognition of dualism.

The "Conventional-Differences" assumption declares that the grades and ingredients of dark magic are distinctive due to the unusual purposes or benefits of those casting destructive spells than those of pure. Destructive spell casting tends to include symbolism that seems unsafe or damaging to individuals. This distinction, essentially perceived in traditional magic, applies to alternative forms of magic as well.

The "Negative-Link" hypothesis declares that both dark and pure magic are entirely distinctive and are accomplished uniquely, even if they reach uniform effects. It is generally seen in fantasy.

The "Unconnected-Theory" declares that dark and pure magic are precisely identical, distinguished only by their end aims and desire.

"Sun/Moon Magic" refers to pure (White) magic as the magical force of the sun, while dark (Black) magic as the magical force of the moon.

Black Magic Practices

Within familiar conventional religion, such as Christianity, there are definite restrictions surrounding grades of magic and witchcraft.

Genuine title spells - Knowing an individual's actual name allows authority over that person.

Immortality rituals - Taoist's state that life is limited and yearning to live past one's life span is not accepted by nature. There is a major concern with immortality spells and rituals. Every spell designed to lengthen one's life is corrupt, particularly if it takes life force from another being to nourish the spell.

Necromancy - This form is determined not as universal dark magic, but as any supernatural power directly connected to death itself; either by way of divination of innards, or the routine of raising the bodies or souls of the fallen.

Curses- A curse (oath) that can be as modest as wishing "misfortune" upon the physical or non-physical being of another.

White Magic

This record is predominantly established on the accounts of Osari the Wise:

Sutra - *"Uttered or recorded command is a slightly distinctive from prayer, while the desire is consequential."*

Protection Magick - *"Symbolizes a hope to safeguard loved ones, kindred or other, therefore, it is extensively pure by nature. It can, however, also be cast in binding or sealing others."*

Weather Magick - *"Invocations, or the like, for storm or warmth; executed by present-time Christianity."*

Health Giving or Exorcism - *"The pure craft of unnatural healing; this was executed by Judaic and Christian enchanters during the olden days and the bible, including Jesus of Nazareth. That is why exorcism is still greatly supportable in both Christianity and Judaism."*

Blessings Invocations - *"Generally the degree of ministers and men of God. Utilizing the divine to magnetize favorable outcomes upon a person."*

Many rituals executed by dark wizards alluded to on television are said to possess views equivalent to Christianity, but in unnatural form. This type of dark magic seems to be generally founded upon religion, but employs distorted conventions to suit the selfish desires of the practitioner. Black wizards might guide a pentagram just as Satanists reverse the Christian cross. Likewise, tainted ceremonies or sacrifice may exchange blood for wine. Viewed from this point of view, the differentiation between dark and pure magic would be uncomplicated.

Grey Magic

Gray magic is a title used to characterize magic not executed for rewarding, moral or divine intentions, yet not evil-minded either.

According to Osari the Wise, grey magic fights shy of generating any form of evil, even if used for favorable results, such as in preventing people from executing evil acts; gray magic embodies all the aims of pure magic, but also works towards purging the world of evil.

A somewhat distinctive value to gray magic, was bestowed by Roy Bowers, a powerful wizard of the 1960s. His craftsmanship involved bewildering, confusing, and baffling individuals in order to gain authority over them; since by doing so, he gains knowledge of them. In his account labeled *"Genuine Witchcraft is defended,"* Bowers claims the following:

> *"One basic tenet of witch psychological grey magic is that your opponent should never be allowed to confirm an opinion about you, but should always remain undecided. This gives you a greater power over him, because the undecided is always the weaker. From this attitude, much confusion has probably sprung in the long path of history."*

From the scripts of Osari The Wise (section 59, page 80)

"I heal, in the face of eradication, in fear of church's reprisal; I heal, bane and abolish; my ways show my fear and respect to the Creator, the great use of his authority and the enduring love for all things living; I am a druid, I am a necromancer, I am a healer and I am a diviner; but nonetheless - I am a White wizard" – Osari the Wise, 1907.

Demons

Nightmare (1800) by Nicolai Abraham Abildgaard
All Rights Reserved

Demons, when looked upon as spiritual beings, may be human, or non-human with distinguishable souls, which at no time occupied a mortal body.

Demon dealings (Demonology) is the systematized inquiry of evil spirits or the dealings with demons. It is an conventional branch of divinity or theology. It links to spiritual entities who are not to be thought of as gods. It deals with well-disposed entities inferior to the rank of Gods, and with vicious entities of all grades and ranks. The early understanding of "demon", was a kind being.

As stated earlier, all the matters of life are under the authority of spirits, linked to the Great Hall of Spirits. Therefore, it is believed that demons are the spirits of those who broken free or exiled.

It should also be expressed that innumerable spirits dwell in the divine; however, a few survive inside the material world. Their chief intention is to bear misplaced spirits from the physical world into the divine.

The Jewish Talmud affirms that there are seven million demons, separated into seventy-two groups. And these demons have authority upon the recently departed. The countless demonic spirits were given charge over the deliverance of fallen spirits into the divine world. The attribution of hostility to the nature of these spirits is by no means all embracing.

Summoning Demons

Ceremonial magicians will aim to compel and control demons to do their bidding, utilizing techniques mentioned in the *Goetia* and *The Book of Abramelin*. The spirits are those spoke of in Christian demonology. These magicians will not worship these demons, but aspire to utilize their know-how to obtain their selfish goals. Others choose to worship, and some look upon their belief as "demonolatry". They recognize the techniques used in the Goetia as "insulting" to the spirits and unsafe for the magician. They alternatively use forms of worship, magick, and rituals which call upon the demons, *imploring* their favor rather than *controlling* them.

THE SEAL OF THE DEMON "HAURES"
(From "Goetia")

The Sixty-fourth Spirit is Haures, or Hauras, or Havres, or Flauros. He is a Great Duke, and appeareth at first like a Leopard, Mighty, Terrible, and Strong, but after a while, at the Command of the Exorcist, he putteth on Human. Shape with Eyes Flaming and Fiery, and a most Terrible Countenance. He giveth True Answers of all things, Present, past, and to Come.

Exorcism

Exorcism is the remarkably life-threatening convention of expelling demons or other spiritual entities from a human being, beast, or dwelling that are possessed by forcing the spirit to assert a verbal curse. The convention is ancient and practiced by enchanters and churchmen since the days of the bible.

Convictions and conventions applying to the system of exorcism are significantly associated with the archaic Dravidians.

The "Atharva Veda" is expressed to include the mysteries associated with magic, charms and medicine. Various practices depicted throughout the text are practical when connected to casting out evil spirits.

In Christian tradition the individual carrying out the exorcism ritual, recognized as an exorcist, is generally a subscriber of the Catholic Church, or a person thought to be blessed with supernatural authorities or abilities. The exorcist can use devotions, and religious texts, such as prescriptions, hand movements, tokens, symbols, talismans, etc. The exorcist will eventually call upon God, or various divine spirits and archangels to assist him. Exorcism is chiefly connected with the Church, while non-Catholics also execute exorcisms.

In general, possessed individuals are not judged as evil, or utterly liable for their conduct. Practitioners often regard exorcism as a cure. The orthodox conventions traditionally take this into account, "overseeing" the procedure to ensure that no bodily harm befall on the possessed, only that they should be secured if potential for violence exists.

The Church clings to the fantasy that exorcism entails the banishment of an "evil spirit," which acquired ownership of a person's physical body. This is rarely the case.
Alternatively, the key intent of exorcism should be to banish the demon back into the angelic world. One must realize that periodic exorcisms carried out by the Catholic Church was "genuinely deceitful," it was used as a device to win over the support of individuals by displaying the "true" authority of the Church and its Christian God.

Concepts of Ceremonial Magic

Ceremonial magic (magick) is a comprehensive expression used within the theme of Hermeticism to embrace a broad variation of lengthy, precise, and complicated magical routines. This form of magic can be perceived as an extension of ritual magick, and in nearly all matters interchangeable with it.

Eliphas Levi

Lévi's translation of magick came to be a considerable accomplishment, particularly following his death. His magical guidance were self-governing from evident fanaticisms, even if they stood rather obscure. Levi merged Tarot cards into his system, and as a consequence the Tarot became a significant piece of the accessories used by witches worldwide.

The Golden Dawn

The Golden Dawn was an influential magical order of the late 19th century, carrying out forms of theurgy and divine growth. It apparently had the finest impact on twentieth century magic. Some characteristics of magic and routine that came to be key essentials of many other conventions, including Wicca, Thelema and additional grades of magical spirituality accepted today, are somewhat taken from the Golden Dawn tradition.

Practicing Ceremonial Magic

The practice of ceremonial magic generally requires instruments manufactured or devoted particularly for this use, which are needed for a special ritual or sequence of rituals. They may be a symbolic model or of supernatural concepts.

The magician is surrounded by these instruments, designed to keep his ambition pure. A Book of Conjurations and Bell are needed, as is the dressing of a Crown, Robe, and Lamen. The crown states the wizard's divinity, the robe represents stillness, and the lamen declare his aim.\

Grimoires

A Grimoire is a secret text of magick. Books of this class give guidance for calling upon angels or demons, carrying out divination and attaining supernatural powers.
Wizards were frequently put on trial by the Christian church, so their diaries remained unseen to prevent them from being destroyed. Such books include astrological communications, lists of angels and demons, instructions on casting spells, on blending remedies, summoning supernatural entities, and manufacturing talismans.

Enochian magic

Enochian magic is a practice of ceremonial magick established upon the summoning and commanding of different demons and spirits. It is founded upon the scripts of Dr. John Dee and Edward Kelley, who insisted that their intelligence was brought forth directly by angles. Dee's diaries included the Enochian texts and the chart of communications that goes with it. It claims to incorporate mysteries embraced within the Book of Enoch.

The Classes

Mages

Mages are a remarkable kind of arcane wizards. They are commonly noted as Mayans, Druids or Celtic, but no compelling proof of their survival exist. Mages guide their focus towards magic that effectively shifts or transforms materiality, generally with the specific goal of harming or healing others or producing "elemental mirages".

Mages believe the mechanism of arcane energy so well that they can practice nearly all grades of magic with celebrated efficiency. A proficient mage who is committed to the specialization of one specific grade of magic becomes more entrenched, and may provoke fiercer outcomes in his spell.

"Magi" is a term, used since the days of the bible, to represent a disciple of Zoroaster, one who can "read" the stars and influence the fate that his reading prophesied.

The Celtic Mages first conquered the crafts of casting spells using the fundamental elements of water and fire. Mages are also recognized for their ability to beckon primitive demons, but that was never substantiated. The finest mortal mage was considered to be Matthew, who some insist is still alive.

Christian say that a band of Mages inspected the infant Jesus shortly after his birth. This convention originates from the Gospel of Matthew. The verses illustrate how a Mage from the east was informed of the birth by the appearance of an unusual star. Upon their coming in Jerusalem, they traveled to King Herod to discover the whereabouts of this child. Herod announced that he had not gotten word of the child, but informed them of a prophecy that the baby Jesus would be born in Bethlehem. The Hermetic Order used the title "Magus" to mention the second-highest grade of skill in their rank system. This system, with related titles.

DRUIDS

A druid was the term bestowed upon the Celtic priests during their last days on this earth. They were brutally suppressed by the Roman Church, and the surviving bands fled and took shelter in the forest, among the evergreens and the primitive creatures who lived there. They faded from written record by the 2nd century, although there were later revivals in Britain and Ireland.

Almost no present-day proof exists, and hence little can be said with regard to the druids with certainty. It is known that they held the cultural repository of comprehension and magical command in an oral tradition, using folklore as a tool to guarantee the communication of magical abilities over time. The fundamental points of druidic convictions was their faith in rebirth, and their custom of human sacrifice. Their proclaimed admiration for various aspects of nature has also been linked to animism.

Druids are stewards of the universe who walked the path of nature, exercise the intelligence of the ancient nature priests, healing and caring for the natural world.

To a druid, nature is a fragile balance of divine actions, in which even the slightest inequality can bend tranquil skies into thundering chaos. Druids gather their authority from this wild power, using it to concoct prevailing grades of magic; they can use their love of nature to dominate its binding powers.

Since their defeat, most surviving druids have submitted to a number of reforms, such as encouraging the investigation of magic from nature totems. Druids who do this are recognized as "druids of the wild."

Shamans

Shamans are holy diviners of eastern tribes. These talented magicians can observe the world of spirits and connect with invisible, supernatural beings. They are tormented by revelations of the approaching and use their visions to advise people during difficult times. Although the shaman may appear clever and composed a flash, he is a formidable magician; when focused, his power is as intense as those who have a bond with God.

Archaeological evidence survived. In November, investigators reported the finding of a 12,000-year-old site in Israel that they believe to be one of the earliest recognized shaman burials. Inside the strange grave they found fifty flawless tortoise shells, a human foot, and certain body parts from animals such as a cow tail and eagle wings. Shamanism has survived since the Egyptian enchanters first uncovered the "command of the elements."

Kabbalists

Kabala is a discipline of thought dealing with the arcane systems of Judaism. It is a set of mystic systems meant to illustrate the connection between the infinite Creator and the limited universe which he created. Kabbalah define the natural world of the world and the individual, the nature and purpose of human life, and many other ontological issues. It also presents methods to grant comprehension of these notions, and to thereby attain divine enlightenment. It was initially developed entirely within the domain of Judaic thought and continually uses traditional Judaic origins to illustrate and manifest its cryptic teachings. These teachings are thus held by Jewish magicians to clarify the concealed significant of the Tanach and conventional Judaic texts, as well as to illustrate the importance of Jewish spiritual customs.

Kabalistic Understanding of God

"The foundation of all foundations, and the pillar of all wisdom is to know that there is God, who brought into being all existence. All the beings of the heavens, and the earth, and what is between them came into existence only from the truth of God's being."

There has been conventional discussion about whether wizards and conjurors initially studied Kabbalah. Jewish system of beliefs examined the limitations of Divine comprehension from man's thought, and disputed man's ability to originate true magic.

In the Kabalistic design, God is neither physical nor spirit, but is the designer of both. The challenge of the Divine universe motivated Kabbalists to view God as the all-knowing "creator", one who preserves the world, and interacts with human beings. Kabbalists speak of God as "Ein Sof"; "the infinite" or "endless". emanations.

Magical Elements of the Torah

The Bible specifies further evidence for magical theory. The soothsayer Ezekiel's sights especially appealed to numerous occult theories. Jacob's vision of the ladder to paradise presented further evidence of obscure knowledge. Moses' encounters with the Burning bush and God on Mount Sinai are an indication of arcane occurrences in the Tanach that shape the foundation of Jewish occult views.

The seventy-two letter name of God, which is used in Judaic mysticism for meditation and reflection aims, is obtained from the words spoken by Moses in the company of an angel.

The Zohar proved to be the leading magical work of Kabbalah, and the most significant. From the thirteenth-century onward, Kabbalah became greatly distributed, and it branched out into far-reaching texts and magical systems. Historians reasoned that the common scrutiny of Judaic esotericism at the time corresponded with, and symbolized a retort to, the increasing authority of the rationalist ideology of Maimonides and his disciples.

The key concepts of magic within the Golden Dawn are largely drawn from the Kabalah and the Zohar. References to the Kabalah can be found throughout the works.

It is the author's individual endorsement that you take it upon yourself to decipher and review the Zohar and the laws depicted in the Kaballah. These reviews are the indispensable key to an all-encompassing comprehension and application of witchcraft and sorcery.

Voodoos

Vaudou is a syncretic religion developed in Haiti. It is founded upon a fusing of the convictions and traditions of West African people, with primitive spiritual beliefs, and Roman Catholic Christianity, which were delivered when African slaves were brought into Haiti in the 16th century and forced to substitute their sacred convictions to those of their masters, while they generally still practiced their conventional African beliefs.
The dominant conviction in Haitian Vodou is that divinities called "Loa" are inferiors to a God called Bondyè, This Supreme Being does not intervene on behalf of human, and it is to the Lwa that Vodou rituals are directed. Other features of Vodou include worship of the departed and safekeeping against witchcraft.

Vodou shares many equivalences to alternative African beliefs, including the Louisiana Voodoo of New Orleans, Santería and Arará of Cuba, and Candomblé and Umbanda of Brazil.

From the scripts of Osari The Wise
(section 145, page 103)

"from the edges of the cosmos, I witness the distinctive types of magic; Judaic charming, Catholic enchantments, Greek Spells, Egyptian Illusions; one bore unequaled, the black Magia of the dark skinned of the east, dark and abolished, consulting ancient evil spirits of the past, those who names shall not be spoken of. This causes me marvel: how did they come across this understanding? What force of God shall suffer a man to sorrow at the pin stoke of a stilted doll?"
– Osari the Wise, 1907.

Wicca

Wicca is a Neopagan religion and a grade of contemporary witchcraft. It is frequently quoted as Witchcraft, by its disciples, who are celebrated as Wiccans or Witches. Its controversial source established in 20th-century England, though it was first made accessible to the general public during the 1950s by Gerald Gardner - who called it the "witch cult" and "religion of witchcraft".

In Wicca, believers worship a Goddess and a God, who are conventionally seen as the Triple Goddess and Horned God. These two divinities are frequently viewed as being aspects of a finer pantheistic Divine, and as establishing themselves as diverse polytheistic gods. Wicca, embraces the ceremonial conventions of magic, largely affected by the ritualistic magick of previous centuries, sometimes in concurrence with an open-minded code of principles recognized as the Wiccan Rede, although this is not supported by all Witches. Another distinctive is the remembrance and observance of seasonally based anniversaries known as Sabbats, of which there are generally eight annually.

Wiccan convictions transform between distinct traditions. However, differing commonalities survive between the many groups, which generally comprise opinions on theology, life after death, magic and conduct. For most Wiccans, both God and Goddess are perceived as perfect contrasts in the world that balance each other out, and in this form, they were contrasted to the notions of yin and yang. The two deities are occasionally granted token symbols, with the Goddess being represented as the Earth, or the Moon, and the God as the Sun.

"The Gods are real, not as persons, but as vehicles of power. Briefly, it may be explained that the personification of a particular type of cosmic power in the form of a God or Goddess, carried out by believers and worshippers over many centuries, builds that God-form or Magical Image into a potent reality on the Inner Planes, and makes it a means by which that type of cosmic power may be contacted."

Traditionally, the wiccan divinity is regarded as a Horned God, united with nature, wilderness, sexual instincts, hunting and the life cycle. Many confuse this God with the conventional Christian image of Satan, who is viewed as being an entity devout to evil and evildoing, in reality, Satan does not exist, nor is he presented in wiccan beliefs or traditions. Contrary to many beliefs, wiccans never worship the Devil, or "Satan".

The Goddess, on the other hand, is a divine deity comprising of a Mother Goddess, associated with maidenhood, virginity, fertility and intelligence. She is also generally portrayed as a Moon Goddess, and is often granted the title of "Diana." Some Wiccans view the Goddess as the more powerful deity, referred to as "the spark of existence and life." This is portrayed in the conventional design of the wiccan coven.

Magic in Wicca

Most Wiccans practice witchcraft in its many forms. Many believe it to be the law of nature, as yet misjudged or ignored by present day science, and as such they do not see it as being paranormal, but being a "part of the supernatural authorities that dwell in the natural" according to some.

> *"The point of magic in Witchcraft] is to make the "bendable" world bend to your will... Unless you possess a rock-firm faith in your own powers and in the operability of your spell, you will not achieve the burning intensity of will and imagination which is requisite to make the magic work." - Paul Huson*

Common Wiccan spells include healing, protection spells, fertility spells, or banishing spells.

> *"Bide the Wiccan laws ye must, in perfect love and perfect trust... Mind the Threefold Law ye should - three times bad and three times good... Eight words the Wiccan Rede fulfill - and it harm none, do what ye will."- Lady Gwen Thompson*

There exists no assertive ethical code followed universally by Wiccans of all conventions; however, many follow a system known as the Wiccan Rede, which states "an it harm none, do what ye will". This is generally translated as a proclamation of the liberty to act, together with the obligation of taking personal accountability for what follows from one's conduct and diminishing wrongdoing to oneself and others.

BOOK OF SHADOWS

In Wicca, there is no divine source such as the Christian Bible or Jewish Torah, although there are definite scriptures and sources that different conventions hold to be significant and impact their beliefs and traditions.

> *"The Book of Shadows is not a Bible. It is a personal cookbook of spells that have worked for the owner. I am giving you mine to copy to get you started: as you gain experience discard those spells that don't work for you and substitute those that you have thought of yourselves." Gerald Gardner to his followers.*

Similar to the grimoires of ceremonial magicians, *The Book of Shadows* incorporates commands and instructions for how to carry out magical rituals and spells, as well as chants and laws of engagement with demons or angels. The original purpose was that every published copy of the Book would be distinct, because a disciple would write their own events and initiators. However, among many Gardnerian Witches today, especially in the western world, all copies of the Book of Shadows are kept identical to the original edition, with nothing being altered. *The Book of Shadows* was initially designed to be kept a secret, but pieces of the Book were published by a number of authors in history.

Today, many adopted the concept of the Book of Shadows, with many solitaries also keeping their own accounts, sometimes including sources taken from the promulgated Gardnerian Book of Shadows. In other practices however, procedures are never written down, meaning that there is no need for a Book of Shadows.

From the scripts of Osari The Wise
(section 3, page 126)

"When I was seeing a confidant in the faint south, I unearthed a new system which worships images of God and exhorts magic, Upon my research, I understood that this fresh system is anything but unjust towards God; in fact, its principal source of rule is symbolized by God himself, in spite of the fact that he is spoken of under an unlike fame and title; it is yet an equivalent origin of life, this is the occult of the Wicca" – Osari the Wise, 1907.

Symbols

Wiccans use different tokens similar to the crucifix or the Star of David. The most notable is the pentagram, which has five edge points each symbolizing one of the five pure forces in Wicca (earth, air, fire, water and spirit); and also the idea that the human, with its five appendages, is a microcosm of the universe. Other symbols and icons used include the triquetra, and the triple Moon symbol of the Triple Goddess.

Most covens are members of wiccan covens. However, there are many solitary wiccans who do not align themselves with any particular lineage, working alone. There are some covens, which do not follow any distinct convention, instead choosing their powers and practices solitarily.

Understanding Wizardry

Wizardry is connected to magical convictions and practices and is the channel with which people supernaturally influence reality through the use of incantations, procedures, or focused thought, in either a destructive or pure way.

Many wizards keep to themselves and do not reveal their existence or identity to the outside world in fear of prosecution, they learned and developed their skills by study of the texts depicted in this book.

A wizard, or an individual recognized under the term, is someone who can tap into the divine and utilize the forces within it; they are familiar characters in the Bible, and it was documented that factual wizards had vanished from the public eye after 1480, when Europe became dominated with witch hunting. Wizards have powers arising from their link to "the source" - the never-ending energy which surrounds us at all times, or as others may refer to it – their ability to connect to God or the divine world.

Wizards, witches and practitioners of magic by other names have appeared in myths, folk tales and published writings throughout recorded history. They generally materialize in fantasy as spiritual leaders or villains, and more recently as heroes. Although they are often depicted as employing great magical powers, their role in shaping the fantasy cosmos they inhabit varies; much of fantasy literature writes of primitive worlds with wizards in a fairly limited role as wardens or advisers.

Punishment for wizardry and witchcraft is spoken of in the earliest law codes preserved. The Code of Hammurabi orders:

"if a man has put a magic spell upon another man, and it is not justified, he upon whom the spell is laid shall go to the holy river; into the holy river he shall he plunged. If the holy river overcomes him, and he is drowned, the man who put the spell upon him shall take possession of his house. If the holy river declares him innocent, and he remains unharmed the man who laid the spell shall be put to death. He who plunged into the river shall take possession of the house of him who laid the spell upon him."

As mentioned earlier, the Hebrew Bible vigorously denounces sorcery. Deuteronomy 18:11-12 calls it an "abomination" and Exodus 22:18 prescribes "thou shalt not suffer a witch to live"; tales like that of 1 Samuel 28, reporting how Saul "hath cut off those that have familiar spirits, and the wizards, out of the land" suggest that in practice, sorcery could at least lead to exile."

Rabbis were reported to have condemned to death 80 women and 35 men, who were accused of witchcraft, on a single day in Ashkelon.

So, one must comprehend that "witchcraft" exists in every religion. Regardless of your individual belief, you are able to make use of unusual forms of magic; the divine plane from which God gives authority to wizards, witches and necromancers still survive and while it was originally designed to be kept hidden, some of this sacred knowledge is available to common folk.

When the Hebrews were dominated in Egypt, they observed the dark secrets of Egyptian magick, which includes the use of incantations and conjurations of ancient Egyptian charms. A well-known use of outlawed Judaic spell is the use of the Pulsa Denura oath aimed towards previous Israeli prime ministers. These curses and spells were taken from 'Sefer ha-Razim'

EXAMPLE OF KNOWN JEWISH SPELL

Pulsa deNura, or "whips of fire" is a cabalistic magic ritual in which the angels of havoc are called upon to destroy a person's soul in the eyes of God, causing all the curses named in the Bible to befall him eventually resulting in his death. However, the Torah forbids the use of such magic. The source for this spell is not to be found in Kabala, but among the Hebrew magical manuals of ancient times, such as Sefer ha-Razim and Harba de-Moshe.

Reportedly, ten Jewish wizards provoked the Pulsa DeNura curse at a grave site near Safed several months prior to the political execution of former Prime Minister Yitzhak Rabin. And yet again, several months prior to the death of Arial Sharon.

You can find the video of the practice on www.How-To-Become-A-Wizard.com

Wizards in History

Confidence in mixed magical systems has magnified in European and Western record, under force from either methodical monotheistic religions or from mental rejection regarding the genuineness of magic, and the superiority of scientism.

Gothic authors, under the command of the Catholic Church, restricted their magic to limited collections of spells. During the early middle Ages, the "trend" of relics as representation of paranormal privilege arose. Magical accounts were told of the magical power of relics to produce wonders, not only to heal the sick, but for purposes like affecting the result of a battle. Tales of these magical relics were collected later into somewhat fashionable works such as the Golden Legend of Jacobus de Voragine or the Dialogus miraculorum of Caesar of Heisterbach.

Magic and Romanticism

Renewed fascination with magic transpired toward the end of the nineteenth-century. Mystics began re-introducing unusual principles to Europeans at this time. New mystic texts and organizations materialized during the nineteenth century. The Golden Dawn evoked the greatest of this "wave" of magic, appealing to luminaries like Aleister Crowley, William Butler Yeats, Algernon Blackwood, and Arthur Machen to its banner.

Magic in the Twentieth Century

A further renewal of curiosity in magic was publicized by the repeal, in England, of the last Witchcraft Act in 1951. This was the incentive for Gerald Gardner, one of the "founders" of modern Wicca, to produce his first book 'Witchcraft Today', in which he professed to uncover the existence of a witch-cult that dated back to pre-Christian Europe. Gardner's new religion integrated magic and religion in a unique way that later provoked people to doubt the boundaries between the two disciplines.

Gardner's unknown religion, and many impersonators, took off in the atmosphere of the 1960s and 1970s, when the counterculture of the "hipsters" also gave rise to another period of reestablished involvement in magic, divination, and other magical practices.

The conventional portrayal of the wizard is depicted as prophet, visionary and master of nature's elements. The wizard is a genius who works with nature to transform himself and others...

Wizards are also perceived as wardens of arcane wisdom and searchers of secret knowledge and truth; they then share that command with their apprentices in order to pass on that sacred comprehension they have obtained. They are feared for their magical power that comes from that skill, and respected for their talent with effects that others cannot readily comprehend.

They keep alive their 'understanding-trust' for unborn generations to "service" the society they serve. They are keepers of human skillfulness, and protectors of applicable intelligence.

Any unnatural effects we create by use of magic or spell could be called "Wizardry" (Including the recently sought-after 'Law of Attraction'). The comprehension and skill we attain to perform this magic can be used in endless ways. Society can benefit from the outcomes we produce and the world becomes a 'magical' place on account of that effort. The Law of Attraction is, in fact, a form of magic.

The prehistoric cosmos was saturated with witchcraft & wizardry. People supported the command of these divine powers. In this ancient past, believers in witchcraft and wizardry had need of those experts, who were capable of changing or remedying matters in the world with a mere utterance of a spell or curse.

Biblical prohibition of wizardry is repeated a number of times. In Deut. 18:10-12, we read:

There shall not be found among you any one that ... use divination, or an observer of times, or an enchanter, or a witch, or a charmer, or a consulter with familiar spirits, or a wizard, or a necromancer, for all that do these things are an abomination unto the Lord.

One, of a few instances, is that of the woman who divined using the Ob. It is told that visited the woman in Ein Dor, who divined using the Ob. She summoned the spirit of the prophet Samuel, who passed not long before, we learn that Saul had murdered all the other diviners, in accordance with the verse, "You shall not suffer a witch to live."

The Bible tells many other stories of women who engaged in witchcraft, and there is even a particular emphasis on women in contrast to men. Although many atheists-occultist and metaphysics professors profess that Moses was a wizard who communicated with God by use of magical abilities.

From the scripts of Osari The Wise
(section 1, page 39)

"A wizard is one who comprehends the actual authorities of his magic, practice his spells and whisperers in confidant, and attain true haera (nirvana) in the face of God the initiator. To be a wizard, you must first have the incessant desire to discover and inform, and to accompany those who practice it expertly. Otherwise, you will barely end up as a ghostly follower of unrevealed secrets" – Osari the Wise, 1907.

Understanding Witchcraft

Similar in form to Wizardry, Witchcraft is the use of similar form of magic, used primarily by those who subscribe to Wicca or other nature religions.

Since the mid-20th century, Witchcraft has become the self-designation of a part of Neopaganism, especially in the Wicca tradition following Gerald Gardner, who claimed a religious tradition of Witchcraft with pre-Christian roots.

Each society has its own distinct body of theories dealing with magic, religion, pure or destructive spirits, and ritual; and these concepts have no self-evident equivalents in other traditions.

Witchcraft is also used to refer to the convention of magic in an uniquely inimical sense. In the past, witches furnished many supernatural "services" in regional communities, if a community welcomes the magical practice, then there is conventionally a clear detachment between swindlers and the terms used to describe legitimate practitioners of witchcraft. The use of 'sorcery, for example, was most often found in accusations against people who were believed of inciting harm in the community by way of magical means. Such witch trials are common for African, Native American, and Asian populations.

Witchcraft was generally connected with heresy, causing great turmoil among Christians. During this time, the notion of witchcraft came progressively to be falsely elucidated as a form of Devil worship. Indictments of witchcraft were frequently integrated with other accusations of atheism against such groups.

In recent years, witchcraft has taken on a distinctly favorable association among Wiccans, as the conventional component of their scriptural convictions.

Whereas witchcraft incorporates the use of magic, there are numerous other forms magic. Witchcraft is well-known in folk magic tales, religious magic, wizardry and ceremonial magic. Progressive wiccans are likely to use the term when speaking of folk magic. The term is also frequently misused when speaking of other forms of magic. In addition to this, many folks oppose the survival of witchcraft and consider every form of magic to be evil.

Wizardry and witchcraft are not the same, but they are similar. Both are involved with provoking effects superior to the natural powers of man by tapping into divine powers.

Practices to which 'witchcraft' applies are those which manipulate a person's flesh or mind against his or her will, or, which are presumed to undermine the social or religious order. Some critics consider the malevolent nature of witchcraft to be a Christian faith.

Many examples can be found in antediluvian texts, where witchcraft and wizardry were believed to have the power to manipulate the natural order of things. Witches were blamed for sickness, disorder, bad luck, sudden death, impotence and other disasters. Wizardry (use of arcane magic) was considered to be more socially acceptable since it was commonly executed by male practitioners, and often in great secret.

Fears of the supernatural generated large-scale witch-hunts in Christian Europe. It was strongly conceived that Christianity engaged in war against the Devil and his legions of witches, who came in alliance. Records indicate tens or hundreds of thousands of "witches" were executed, and others were incarcerated, tormented, banished, and had lands and property impounded. The greater part of those accused were women, though in some regions the majority was men. Allegations of witchcraft were integrated with other accusations of blasphemy. .

The Malleus Maleficarum, a renowned witch-hunting guidebook used by the Catholic Church, outlines how to recognize a witch, the qualities of a witch, how to put a witch to trial and how to punish a witch. The book describes a witch as wicked.

While witches and wizards commanded respect, public impressions of them were often conflicting, many were feared. Throughout Europe, many healers (who were not titled "Christians" or empowered by the Catholic Church) were convicted of witchcraft. Healers, wise-man, prophets, and non-suspecting individuals were accused of witchcraft and condemned for death. This resulted in the desertion of witchcraft over time and the public exercise of any authority that could be interpreted as "Devil-dealing".

Some diviners considered themselves "agents" of the spiritual worlds, roughly comparable to shamans. Some witches became proficient in necromancy, which is the dark practice of connecting with the spirits of the dead for aims of divination or prophecy – although the title has also been assigned to the beckoning of dead bodies for other purposes. The Biblical *Witch of Endor* is presumed to have accomplished it (1 Sam. 28), and it is one of the many magical traditions condemned by Ælfric of Eynsham:

Current scholarly estimates of the number of people executed for witchcraft vary between about 40,000 and 100,000. The total number of witch trials in Europe, which are known for certain to have ended in executions, is around 12,000. In Early Modern European tradition, witches have stereotypically, though not exclusively, been women. European pagan belief in witchcraft was associated with the Goddess Diana and dismissed as "diabolical fantasies" by medieval Christian authors. Witch-hunts first appeared in large numbers in southern France and Switzerland during the 14th and 15th centuries. The peak years of witch-hunts in southwest Germany were from 1561 to 1670.

The popularity of necromancy gave rise to the outrage and wrath of Christianity, which came to be the governing force in Europe, and concern with necromancy (and magic) dwindled. The most famed conflict between witchcraft and state took place in Salem. The witch trials were a series of trials to punish those accused of witchcraft. Over fifty men and women were killed during that time.

Hebrew Bible

References to sorcery (Keshef) in Jewish history are common, and the fierce condemnations found there are based upon the abomination of the black art in itself.

The Hebrew Bible grants some proof that magical teachings were prosecuted under the Hebrew kings:

> *And Saul disguised himself, and put on another raiment, and he went, and two men with him, and they came to the woman by night: and he said, I pray thee, divine unto me by the familiar spirit, and bring me, him up, whom I shall name unto thee. And the woman said unto him, Behold, thou knowest what Saul hath done, how he hath cut off those that have familiar spirits, and the wizards, out of the land: wherefore then layest thou a snare for my life, to cause me to die? - The Hebrew verb Hichrit, translated in the King James as cut off, can also be translated as excommunicate, or as kill wholesale or exterminate.*

Jewish law views the convention of witchcraft as being overloaded with ungodliness and idol worship; it is admitted that while magic exists, it is prohibited to exercise it on the premise that it generally requires the adoration of other Gods. Rabbis of the Talmud also denounced magic when it provoked anything but illusions. However, many Rabbis exercised magic themselves.

Present-day witchcraft often includes the use of divination, magic, and working with the harmonious earthly elements and obscure forces such as the forces of nature. The procedure of natural medicine, folk medicine, and spiritual healing is also common, as are alternative medical and New Age healing practices. Some schools of modern witchcraft, such as traditional forms of Wicca, are secretive and operate as initiatory secret societies.

Understanding Necromancy

  Necromancers are mortal practitioners of "fatality magic", also known as Black Magia. They channel their command of the arcane into manipulation of the authorities of life and death.

  They are "Spell Casters" whose black art manipulates the sovereignty of death. In calling upon this force, necromancers risk being devoured by it — until ultimately, they unite with the agents of death.

  Communicating with dead spirits, is an ancient and revered magical tradition and is an undivided part of nearly all shamanic beliefs. Some progressive religions (Shinto and Santeria) still practice the form, for the purpose of contacting and sacrificing to ancestral spirits and Gods.

  Necromancy is an exceptional grade of divination by the summoning of the dead (Known also as Nigromancy). The particulars and circumstances of these dealings with departed spirits — such as time, place, and ceremonies to be followed.

Along with other grades of divination and magic, necromancy is found in nations of ancient times, and is a convention common to paganism at all times and in all countries, but nothing certain can be said as to the place of its source. Necromancers bend arcane magic to influence the power of "Malach Ha Mavet" (Angel of Death). Commanding the dead, commonly by using incantations and powerful charms, they progressively take on many of the idiosyncrasies of demons, or the Archangel of Death himself.

In the bible, Moses warned the Israelites against mimicking the Chanaanite abominations, among which attempting to discover the truth from the dead is alluded to. The summoning of the dead took place specifically in large caves, burial grounds, in regions of mass wreckage or disaster, or near rivers and lakes, where the dealings with the dead was thought to be easier.

The Mosaic Law claims that to seek information from the deceased is forbidden by God, and even makes it punishable by death. Nonetheless, due to the use of Judaic books during Necromantic ceremonies (such as Harba de Moshe, The Zohar),we find it practiced by banished Hebrews of old. Especially during the time of Saul, who forcefully reprimanded them on this ground, and of Manasses. The best-known case of necromancy in the Bible is the summoning of the soul of Samuel at Endor (1 Samuel 28).

The Process

Necromancy is a complicated practice used since ancient times by very enlightened conjurors; only the fearless, undismayed and solitary conjuror has any possibility of success in such a undertaking.

It was repeatedly said to be immoderately unsafe; for not only is a bond with the dead required, but by absorbing and granting life-energies, one come in enduring union with the mischievous link between "body" and "soul." Thus, unless he has taken exceptional precautions, the necromancer could be in great jeopardy.

To awaken the dead, the necromancer needs to attain the aid of potent spirits, both for his own protection and to influence the spirit to surrender to his will. Spells and rituals found in the Zohar can call upon the commands of spirits. However, one must remember, the beckoning of a spirit may result in more than just a mere relinquishment of your own spirit to a fallen angel, but may also bring about haunting and perturbing hallucinations.

Carefully planned groundwork should involve a prudent research of the Zohar and the rituals included in its texts, understanding of Harba de Moshe, Razim, Raziel, Goetia and other books of a similar nature.

The site for the undertaking has to be selected with great care; the most promising is a place remote from the living, a lonely road, a cave, a ruin, a deserted forest, or a cursed moor.

Once a time is determined upon for the operation, a series of concentric spheres of influence must be drawn on the surface, within which are the inscribed symbols together with the sacred titles of God. The circle must be venerated and blessed with the necromancer and his apprentice standing at its core, shielded by a ring, and the divine names of God. Then, wand (or staff) in hand, the necromancer calls upon the dead to rise, using the selected ceremony found in the *Goetia* or book of choice.

Experienced necromancers have advocated the need for some effort at identification between the necromancer and the spirit which he is invoking. In his evocation, the necromancer will beckon the spirit or demon by name and, if successful, he has to deal with the petrifying anguish of a spirit shrieking and muttering with wrath at having been forced to return to its former life. Occasionally, the dead comes forth in the forms of fierce creatures wrathful of the necromancer and his self-serving use of anomalous powers.

When the spirit or demon ultimately bends to the necromancer's will, it frequently materializes in pure figure, prepared to answer the questions brought before him by the necromancer.

After the operation, it is required to release the spirit, who commonly evaporates amid clouds of sulphur. Under no circumstances should the necromancer leave the guardianship of the circle before releasing the spirit.

The whole undertaking is fraught with grave perils, for the slightest divergence from the written ceremonies could bring about the undoing of the necromancer and lead to unimaginable mental and physical suffering.

Divination by an aid of the spirits is said to have been conventional among the Celtics and later among the Egyptians, Greeks and Romans as well.

CHAPTER 2
THINK

Get ready to Think

Please know that if you are to investigate the secrets of magic, you will need to be utterly committed to your goal. You will be compelled to keep a receptive and open mind and be willing to reform your beliefs and points of view with regard to religion, and the authorities of creation.

Reading Materials

In learning magic, one's curiosity may lead to the skilled application of the many ceremonies, and rituals of magic. The authorities of spoken words and particular ceremonies are disclosed in what is known as The Grimoire.

Whether by intend or coincidence, The Grimoire is the recorded legacy of the wizard. It consists of the many symbols, procedures and incantations of its owner. The Grimoire is more than just a guide book - it is a reflection of the wizard's past communication with all forms of magic.

> *"Some books cannot be opened with impunity. Enlightenment such-as-this is a loss of innocence, for you cannot unlearn Magick nor-then live in a fool's paradise; blind to good & evil or deaf from truth... this adventure is one-way... crossing the threshold of ignorance and shedding the veil of convention... prepare to see great things... prepare to experience your magnificent self..." -Oliver I. Spence*

In addition to The Grimoire, there are many other books, text and archaic scrolls, which will serve as magic manuals. This chapter supplies further facts with regard to the fundamental books that every wizard, witch or necromancer must read. Please, take notice.

Books of the Kabbalah

Kabala (as acknowledged previously) is an expression of mysticism. It consists of meditative, philosophical, sacred, arcane and magical practices, which were lectured only to a select few; and for this reason, Kabala is considered as a cryptic branch of Judaic magic. The spelling Kabbalah is used to differentiate the diversity of Kabbalah used by western or hermetic magicians from conventional Jewish Kabbalah.

One of the most significant Kabalistic books, the *"Sepher ha Zohar"*, was made known by Moses de Leon. The "Zohar" is a series of independent documents examining a wide range of magical and supernatural disciplines. The "Zohar" has been widely read and was greatly influential within conventional Judaism, as well as Hermetic Kabala.

Old Hermetic Kabala

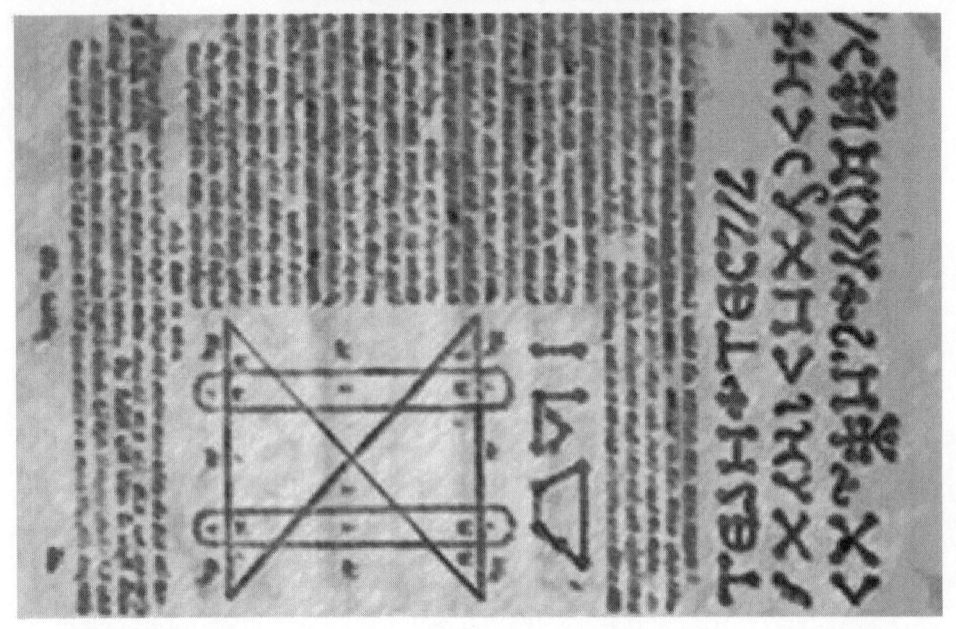

During the 16th century, Western European intellectuals began taking interest in the Kabala. In this century, we first see reports pointing to Hermes Trismegistus, the "father" of Hermetic Magic.

Kabala was a subject of research for most Ceremonialists between the time of John Dee and the Hermetic Order of the Golden Dawn. However, Eliphas Levi, whose impact on the Order of the Golden Dawn and on Thelema was great, rooted his Transcendental Magic (Dogme ET Rituel de la Haute Magie) in a Kabalistic tradition. His principles of the Kabala remains a fundamental text for the student of ceremonial magic.

It would not be hyperbole to claim that the Hermetic Order of the Golden Dawn was a Kabalistic society. Its inaugural framework was based on the Tree of Life. Indeed, its entire magical system depended on this Kabala.

Book of Gematria

777

AND OTHER
QABALISTIC
WRITINGS
OF
ALEISTER
CROWLEY

Gematria is a system of exegesis used, since the olden time of the Second Temple, to obtain insights into the divine writings, to obtain clarifications of the text, or to interpret a profane subject.

The goal is to navigate the incomprehensible Qabalistic interpretation of any magical scriptures. With use of this noteworthy book, you will learn to decode the clues concealed in any holy writ or archaic text.

The Book of the Law

The religion known as Thelema was founded with the publication of *The Book of the Law*. It was received by Aleister Crowley in Cairo, in the year 1904. It consists of three parts, each of which was recorded in one hour, on April 8th, 9th, and 10th. Crowley affirms that the initiator was a demon named Aiwass, whom he later acknowledged as his own keeper. The teachings within this book are clearly communicated in the Law of Thelema, conveyed by these two phrases:

"Do what thou wilt shall be the whole of the Law" (AL I: 40) and *"Love is the law, love under will"* (AL I: 57)

Book of the Dead

The Book of the Dead is the popular title for the antediluvian Egyptian text *The Book of Coming Forth by Day*. The title was conceived by the Richard Lepsius, who printed a collection of the texts in 1842.

The name is slightly deceptive, as the "book" was not a real book. The text was originally fashioned on the surface of a sarcophagus, but was later written on Cyperus papyrus and planted inside the mummy case with the deceased, to keep it hidden.

It constituted a collection of spells, charms and magical procedures for use by the departed in the afterlife, illustrating many of the fundamental teachings of Egyptian sorcery. Knowledge of these spells is the key to understanding the 'method' in which spells and charms are formulated.

Sefer Yetzirah

Yetzirah (*Book of Creation*) is the title of the earliest existing book on Jewish esotericism.

The Sefer Yetzirah is devoted to the understanding of God and the formation of the physical and non-physical world. The ascription of its authorship to Abraham proves its importance. It is said that this work had a greater impact on the evolution of magic than almost any other book after the publication of the Talmud.

All the supernatural achievements attributed to rabbis of the Talmudic era, are ascribed by rabbinic commentators to the use of this book. Abraham was known to be the recipient of the divine realization of magic; so no one ever doubted that Abraham was the original author of this book.

The Sefer Yetzirah is extremely difficult to comprehend because of its cryptic style. The hardship is rendered still greater by the lack of a analytical copy, the present text being much interpolated and altered. Hence, there is a wide variation of opinion with regard to the age, origin, contents, and value of the book. This book is without question the oldest and most mysterious of all Kabbalistic texts.

Prudent study reveals that it is a true magical book. It is said that ancient wizards used this book to "create" living organisms, including demons, golems and elemental entities. The Sefer Yetzirah is very concise, only 2500 words long. The first chapter examines the Sefirot; The second chapter is a review of the letters of the Hebrew alphabet, and the 231 gates; Chapters three to five talk about the classes of the letters in relation to astrology.

The text was intentionally written in code, to ensure that only authentic wizards could read it. Some rabbis took it upon themselves to translate it, and make it accessible for the very first time to English speakers without a Kabbalistic education.

Sefer Raziel HaMalakh
(Spells & Amulets)

Sefer Raziel HaMalakh (Book of Raziel the Angel) is a magical Grimoire, initially written in Aramaic.

The tradition around the book attributes it to Adam, who the book was given to by the angel, Raziel. The title itself is reported in another magical work of ancient times, *The Sword of Moses*.

This Grimoire contains five Books which uncover such secrets as, the secrets of creation, the formation of magical talismans, the angels, the Zodiac, Gematria and the names of God. It draws heavily on the Sepher Yetzirah and *Sepher Ha-Razim*.

However, it is forbidden to open the book or read it because of its inherent power. Therefore, many keep their copies sealed.

Sepher Ha-Razim

Synagogue mosaic showing zodiacal signs for the months of the Hebrew calendar (Bet Alpha Synagogue, Israel).

The Sepher Ha-Razim is a Kabalistic text purportedly given to Noah by the angel Raziel. To say that it is an unconventional text is an understatement; while conventional Judaic laws of purity are part of the cosmology. It is a sourcebook for Judaic magic, calling upon angels, rather than God, to perform magical feats.

Book of the Bahir

The Bahir is one of the oldest and most significant of all Kabbalistic texts. Until the publication of the Zohar, the Bahir was the most instrumental source of Kabbalistic teachings. It is referred to in nearly every major Kabbalistic work and is cited numerous times by the Ramban in his commentary on the Torah. It is also paraphrased and quoted many times in the Zohar.

One of the most consequential notions uncovered in it is that of the "ten Sefirot". Also examined are the opening verses of Genesis and their true meaning; The magical aspects of the Hebrew alphabet; A discussion of reincarnation; The 32 paths of Wisdom, and the Tzimtum, among other topics.

Emerald Tablet

The Emerald Tablet is a brief text considered to be the foundation of the Hermetic movement, and essential to the secret Art of Alchemy. Alchemical writings occasionally reference it by an alternative title: The Secret of Hermes. Its presumed author is Hermes the Thrice-Great, a renowned Egyptian adept named after the Greek God of occult understanding. The source of the Emerald Tablet is long forgotten, and there is no recorded history as to its place of origin. A Latin copy of the Emerald Tablet was contained among the alchemical essays of Isaac Newton. The text was in Newton's own hand.

Carl Jung acknowledged "The Emerald Tablet" as a board made of green stone that he came across in the first of a set of visions beginning at the end of 1912, and climaxing in his writing the Seven Sermons to the Dead in 1916. The ideas incorporated in the Hermetic text are consistent with the enantiodromian processes, characteristic of Jungian individuation.

THE LESSER KEYS OF SOLOMON

The Lesser Key of Solomon, is a mysterious Grimoire, and one of the most widespread books of demonology. It has also long been famously known as the Lemegeton. It materialized during the 17th century, but much was taken from earlier texts, including the Pseudomonarchia Daemonum, and late-medieval grimoires. It is likely that books by Jewish cabalists were also inspirations. Some of the evidence in the first section, concerning the evocation of demons, dates back to the 14th century, or earlier.

The Lesser Key of Solomon includes comprehensive accounts of spirits and the conjurations required to summon and command them to do the will of the conjurer. It details the defensive symbols and ceremonies to be performed, the actions required to hinder the spirits from gaining control, the preparations prior to the invocations, and commands on how to make the essential tools for the accomplishment of these rituals. The several original published copies vary significantly in great detail and in the currect spellings of the spirits' names. Present day editions are vastly attainable in print and on the Internet.

From the scripts of Osari The Wise
(section 112, page 6)

"Upon the beckoning of the great duke demon Gusion, I understood that one need not see tomorrow to know what it beholds; Gusion is an honorable and decorous demon and consulting him will be to your benefit; reading the goetia and following the practices in it, will grant you entry to his wisdom" – Osari the Wise, 1907.

The 72 Demons

The demons' names are taken from the Ars Goetia, which varies in terms of numbers and rankings from the Pseudomonarchia Daemonum of Weyer. As the result of multiple interpretations, there are numerous spellings for some of the titles, which are given in the articles concerning them.

GRIMOIRE SYMPATHIA

A rare guide to the spiritual nature of plants, minerals, and valuable stones for the empathic remedial of the physical body by using symbols, tokens, invocations, chants, aura, and the command of the will; This work is rather extraordinary, being a Grimoire of the spirits of plants, minerals and precious stones. The spirit for each has a title, a sigil and an invocation and these are used for healing purposes.

The spirit qualities were obtained by clairvoyant examination, though the author is recognized to be familiar with Culpeper. However, this is not to be confused with herbalism. The plants are not acquired or used to prepare medication; rather, the sorcerer adapts to their powers to call upon pure forms of nature magic. Very few original, complete Grimoires were published throughout the 20th Century.

Practice of Magical Evocation

Throughout history, many magical accounts were published, but generally in unreliable and fragmentary form.

Throughout history, comprehension and exercise of magic was frequently condemned by many god-fearing orders. During the modern age, magic was considered as pure illusion, and any individual claiming to practice it was scorned. Mystical cults, and others, were accountable for the bad reputation of magic and witchcraft.

True magic was instructed in the oldest divinatory institutes and in hidden movements, to which only few had access. The insignificant number of accounts imparting inadequate knowledge on magic were composed in such a fashion, that their contents would offer little genuine knowledge and understanding of the craft.

The following contain collections of high-powered magic knowledge, spells and ceremonies from either uncommon or eradicated sources. All of these rare collections incorporate genuine conceptions, which should be practiced meticulously and judiciously.

- Century of spells
- Introduction to magic
- Ancient Christian magic
- Magic shield
- Grimoire Of Armadel
- Book of black magic
- Book of sacred magic of Abramelin the mage
- Magick, Book 4, Parts I - IV -Revised
- Techniques of high magic
- Compendium Of Herbal Magick
- John Dee's Five Books Of Mystery
- Black Pullet
- Karanina's Book of Spells
- 21 Spells of Domesius

- Ancient Conjurations and Invocations
- Potent Protection Spells
- Book of Shadows
- Practical Candleburning Rituals: Spells and Rituals for Every Purpose
- Charms, Spells, and Formulas
- Spell Crafts: Creating Magical Objects
- Complete Book Of Spells, Ceremonies & Magic
- The Good Spell Book: Love Charms, Magical Cures, and Other Practical Sorcery
- Book of Spells, The
- Tarot Spells
- Wizard's Spell Compendium, Vol. 1
- Moon Magick: Myth & Magic, Crafts & Recipes, Rituals & Spells
- Spells for the Solitary Witch
- Crone's Book Of Charms & Spells
- Everyday Tarot Magic: Meditation & Spells
- The Salem Witches Book Of Love Spells: Ancient Spells from Modern Witches

Alphabets, Language, and Magic

Human beings use the "writing system" to symbolize uttered language. The forms of the characters embodying an alphabet are often compared to things real or imagined. A self-evident illustration of this case is the English letter "S" which echoes the symbol of a snake, which produces that same sound. Other alphabet shapes are not as evident or may have been tainted as civilizations and their languages developed over the years, but nevertheless, the connections are there.

Many are familiar with the Runic alphabet, but there are a number of other alphabets or scripts associated with witchcraft, charms, spells, and magical or spiritual practices.

In the following pages, you will study these alphabets in their integrality with their parallel English letters, but it is essential to remember that these scripts were given English equivalents based upon the pronunciation of each letter — not because there is a conclusive link between some time-worn language and contemporary English. In other words, when one writes an English word in runes, it is different, as if one were to write as the archaic Norse wrote. You will notice as you inspect the magic alphabet, that many are missing English letters; this is not an error; some of the older languages had no equivalent symbols for all the letters used in our modern-day languages.

Alphabets were originally developed by the Ancients to symbolize magical entities or concepts. Later, they were used for divine writings and ultimately for everyday use. The characterizations of the alphabets that follow have endured through time or have been found again.

BOBILETH ALPHABET

| a | b | c | d | e | f | g | h | i/j | k | l | m |

| n | o | p | q | r | s | t | u/v | w | x | y | z |

full stop / period

This is, in all likelihood, the earliest known pre-Roman writing. In the islands of what would become the area of Britain and Scandinavia, was a Gaelic alphabet known as Ogham, which was first spoke of in the Book of Ballymote. Goidelic comprised of a number of vertical strokes, standing on, suspended from, and crossing one line. After the Ogham, came the Bobileth, or Boibel-Loth alphabet and its derivatives, all preferred to some extent by the Druids in certain areas.

The Enochian

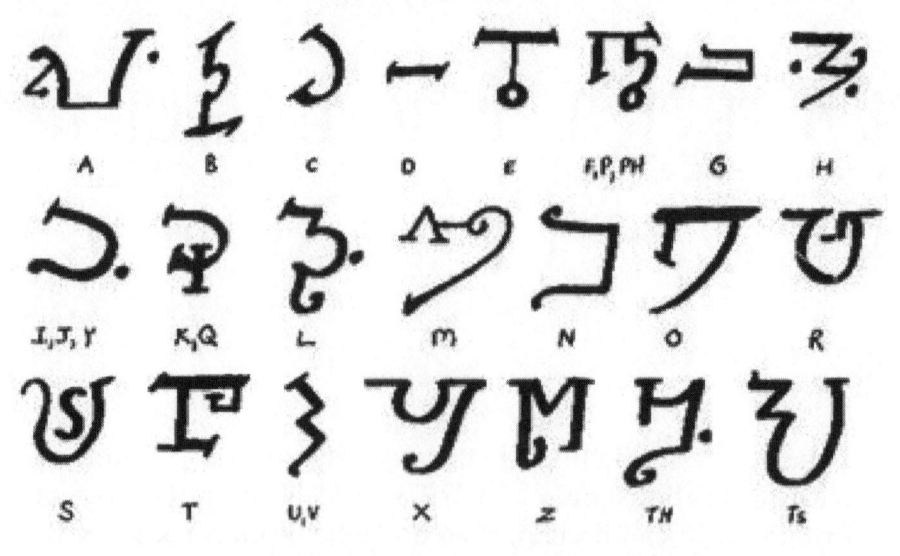

The Enochian alphabet, and the language written with it, was communicated to Dr. John Dee and his companion, Sir Edward Kelly by divine angels. The unique characters shown consisted of the proper alphabet for the Enochian Tablets. The Enochian language is the only known acceptable language for the Enochian Calls, or Keys, which are used to call upon the angels. Therefore, it is a basic in the custom of true Enochian Magic.

The Enochian alphabet shapes the foundation for magical text and language metaphysician, and mathematician John Dee received it from an angel. Dee recorded that the letters expressed the order of man's creation. The Enochian language shaped the basis for an undeveloped theurgical procedure begun by Dee, but never accomplished. Eventually, the Enochian alphabet and language came to be the foundation of the Golden Dawn's magical system until forsaken by Paul Case, due to his belief in the fundamental menace of such system.

The Enochian alphabet contains twenty-one letters, and the language, like Hebrew and other angelic alphabets, is written right to left. Some letters symbolize numerous sounds, including some overlap.

Futhark

ᚠᚢᚦᚨᚱᚲᚷᚹᚾᚺᛁᛃᛇᛈᛉᛊᛏᛒ
f u th a r c/ch g' w h n i j ei p x s t b

ᛖᛗᛚᛜᛟᛞᚫᛦᛠᛣᚸᚷᛥ
e m l ng oe d a' y ea io k g" g st

Futhark is a writing system of uncertain origin that was used by the Germanic people of northern Europe, Britain, Scandinavia, and Iceland from about the 3rd century CE to the 16th or 17th century CE. Because of its angular letterforms, runic writing is believed to belong to an ancient system. Elder Futhark is the oldest form of the runic alphabet, used by Germanic tribes for Proto-Norse and other Migration period; Germanic dialects of the 2nd to 8th century CE are used for inscriptions on artifacts such as jewelry, amulets, tools, and weapons, and also on rune stones. In Scandinavia, the script of the Elder Futhark was simplified to that of the Younger Futhark from the late 8th century CE, while the Anglo-Saxons and Frisians extended the Futhark, which eventually became the Anglo-Saxon Futhorc after Proto-English.

Futhark was likely adapted by the Greek. Futhark can be written either left-to-right or right-to-left. The Futhark of 24 letters is called **"Elder Futhark"**. It was used mostly before the 9th century CE.

As languages changed and additional Germanic groups adopted them, Futhark changed to suit the language when it came to writing. An early offshoot of Futhark was employed by the Goths, and so came to be known as the Gothic Runes. The Gothic Runes were used until 500 CE, when they were replaced by the Greek-based Gothic alphabet.

Futhark and, more specifically, runes have always been seen as possessing mystical properties. Many modern Wiccan sects use Runes ceremonially and ritualistically. As Runes date from before the time Northern Europe became Christianized, they became associated with "pagans" of the non-Christian past and subsequently, a mystique developed around them. Even the supposed root of rune- the German word, raunen- means "to whisper".

Elder Futhark runes are believed to have originated in the Old Italic alphabets. The angular shapes of the runes, presumably an adaptation to the incision in wood or metal, are a property that is shared with other early alphabets, including the Old Italic ones. The runes of uncertain derivation may be original innovations, or adoptions, of otherwise unneeded Latin letters.

The invention of the Futhark script has been ascribed to a person, or persons who had come into contact with Roman culture, perhaps as mercenaries in the Roman army, or even as merchants. The Futhark script was clearly designed for epigraphic purposes, but opinions differ in stressing magical, practical, or graffitical aspects.

ETRUSCAN

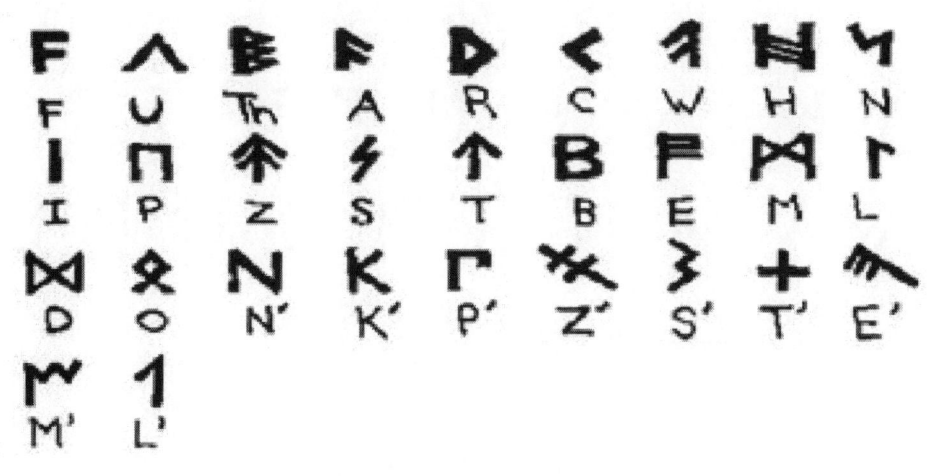

F	ᐱ	ᛒ	F	D	<	ᐃ	H	ᛉ
F	U	Th	A	R	C	W	H	N
I	⊓	✦	ᛋ	↑	B	F	⋈	ᚱ
I	P	Z	S	T	B	E	M	L
⋈	⚘	N	K	Γ	✴	⟩	+	⋀
D	O	N'	K'	P'	Z'	S'	T'	E'
ᛙ	ᚹ							
M'	L'							

The source of the Etruscan alphabet is an engaging development of a language. The first alphabet was designed by Semitic-speakers in the antediluvian Near East. The Canaanite and later Phoenician alphabets had only consonants and no vowels. The Greeks derived their alphabet from the Phoenician alphabet and added vowels, thereby producing the first true alphabet. The Greeks brought a western form of the Greek alphabet to Italy, and the Etruscans acquired the alphabet from them. The Etruscans then passed their alphabet to the Romans.

The alphabet was brought to Italy by Euboean Greeks; the earliest known Etruscan inscription dates back to the middle of the 6th century BCE. The majority of Etruscan inscriptions are written in horizontal lines from left to right, but some are boustrophedon (running alternately left to right then right to left). The Etruscan language was spoken by the Etruscans in Etruria (Tuscany and Umbria) until about the 1st century CE. The emperor Claudius (10 BCE - 54 CE) wrote a 20 volume history of the Etruscans, but none of them have survived. Used in religious ceremonies until the early 5th century, Etruscan is related to Raetic and to Lemnian. The Etruscan alphabet was diffused at the end of the archaic period, around 500 CE, into Camunic, a language once spoken in the northwest of Italy, and became the model for the alphabets of the Alpine populations.

Gothic

𐌰 𐌱 𐌲 𐌳 𐌴 𐌿 𐌶 𐌷 𐌸 𐌹
𐌺 𐌻 𐌼 𐌽 𐌾 𐌽 𐍀 𐍂 𐍃
𐍄 𐍅 𐍆 𐍇 𐍉 𐍁 𐍈

The Goths were one of the most known barbarian tribes accountable for the ruin of the Roman Empire and the civics of early Medieval Europe. The Goths coined their language using their interpretation of the Futhark alphabet, but it was considered a magickal design. Except for a few Norse engravings in runes, records of Gothic are older than those for any other Germanic language.

    The Gothic alphabet was used in all documents written in Gothic and found in Europe. It is conventionally conceived that the Gothic alphabet's 27 letters, comprising of 25 adapted Greek symbols and two runes, were conceived by Ulfilas, a Greek champion accountable for the "conversion" of many Goths to Christianity. His discovery of the Gothic alphabet took the Greek alphabet, added letters from Latin and Futhark alphabets, and formulated new letters to write the Gothic language. The alphabet was used until the 6th century, and was only written in the Gothic language. Many 6th century western wizards used this tongue to cloak their undertakings for the use of magick.

Greek and Hebrew Alphabets

ט	ח	ז	ו	ה	ד	ג	ב	א
Tet (T)	Chet (Ch)	Zayin (Z)	Vav (V/O/U)	He (H)	Dalet (D)	Gimel (G)	Bet (B/V)	Alef (Silent)

ס	ן	נ	ם	מ	ל	ך	כ	י
Samech (S)	Nun (N)	Nun (N)	Mem (M)	Mem (M)	Lamed (L)	Khaf (Kh)	Kaf (K/Kh)	Yod (Y)

ת	ש	ר	ק	ץ	צ	ף	פ	ע
Tav (T/S)	Shin (Sh/S)	Resh (R)	Qof (Q)	Tzade (Tz)	Tzade (Tz)	Fe (F)	Pe (P/F)	Ayin (Silent)

This is a generally used table of Greek and Hebrew alphabet, which have numerical values. Both Greek and Hebrew have only one set of characters used for both words and numbers. When a word in Greek, for example, is written out, it has a mathematical value. This value is called the Gematria.

The Greek alphabet is extracted from the Hebrew alphabet; the Phoenician and Hebrew languages are very closely related; like dialects of one language.

The titles of the Greek letters have their origins in Phoenician and Hebrew. They come from pictographs where the letters were originally derived by simplification. "Aluph" means bull (derived from a bull pictogram), "bet," means house (from the Hebrew "bayt"), "Gamma" comes from "Gammal", meaning camel, and so on. The Greeks added new letters that come after Tau.

Magical Languages

The execution of magic generally requires the use of language. Whether uttered or unuttered, words are commonly used to acquire or direct divine power. In *The Magical Power of Words*, S. J. Tambiah claims that the link between language and magic is due to a conviction in the natural capacity of uttered (or written) words to influence the physical universe. It is recognized that the command of the right words, relevant utterances and the more highly-developed forms of speech, give a man powers above and beyond his own restricted sphere of physical action.

Magical tongue can be seen as a ceremonial act, and could be presented as the equivalent to the implementation of magic ceremonies. However, speech on its own cannot be considered magical. Only certain words and phrases (when spoken in a specific context) could be considered to have magical powers. Magical language, is separate from "scientific" language because it is emotive, and it transforms words into symbols for emotions; whereas in scientific language, words are linked to particular values. Magical language is therefore, exceptionally proficient at designing emotional symbols that link magical practices to the world. The mother tongue of magic is sacred, set and used for a completely different aim to that of ordinary language. The two grades of language are distinguished through the choice of words, use of grammar, style, or by the use of definite clauses or forms: prayers, spells, songs, blessings, or chants. Divine styles of language often utilize archaic words and forms in an effort to appeal to one's purity, or "truth".

Another unrealized origin of the power of words is their clandestineness and exclusivity. Much divine language is distinguished from conventional language, that it is incomprehensible to the majority of the population, and it can only be used and decoded by specialized wizards. Disciples of magic are still able to use and merit the magical function of words, by conceiving in the magical power of the words themselves, and in the meaning that they must bestow upon those who comprehend them.

You can practice magic in any language. However, to practice particular charms and distinctive forms of magic, you will need to comprehend the speech. Otherwise, you may get unusual results.

LATIN

Archaic Latin relates to the Latin language in the era prior to the age of Classical Latin; that is, all Latin before 75 BC. The term "Prisca Latinitas" differentiates New Latin and present-day Latin from vetus Latina, in which "old" has another meaning. It is used in numerous Christian invocations and healing ceremonies, such as the invocation to St. Michael the Archangel.

Sumerian

Sumerian was the language of ancient Sumer, spoken in southern Mesopotamia, since at least the 4th millennium BCE. Sumerian is a sacred, ceremonial, literary and magical. It was unremembered until the 19th century, when Assyriologists began decoding the wedge-shaped engraved tablets left by those who spoke it. Sumerian is considered a "god-forsaken" language.

The Sumerian tongue is the earliest known written language. Records are exclusively logographic, with no linguistic or phonological content. It is recognized that as early as 2500 BC, the Sumerians could deal with unfamiliar forms of magic.

Aramaic

#	Style Name	Aramaic Script
1	Tur Abdin	ܐܒܪܝܐ ܡܠܟܐ
2	Edessa	ܐܒܪܝܐ ܡܠܟܐ
3	Antioch	ܐܒܪܝܐ ܡܠܟܐ
4	Midyat	ܐܒܪܝܐ ܡܠܟܐ
5	Nisibin	ܐܒܪܝܐ ܡܠܟܐ
6	Quenneshrin	ܐܒܪܝܐ ܡܠܟܐ
7	Osroene	ܐܒܪܝܐ ܡܠܟܐ
8	Eastern	ܐܒܪܝܐ ܡܠܟܐ
9	Urhoy	ܐܒܪܝܐ ܡܠܟܐ
10	Assyrian	ܐܒܪܝܐ ܡܠܟܐ

Aramaic is a Semitic tongue with a 3,000-year history. It has been the language of the administration of empires, and the language of godlike worship. It was the common language spoken in Israel during the Second Temple period; the original language of large sections of the Biblical Books of Daniel and Ezra, are likely to have been the mother tongue of Jesus of Nazareth, and is the main language of the Talmud.

Modern Aramaic is uttered today as a first language by many dispelled, predominantly small, and largely detached colonies of varying Christian, Jewish and Muslim societies of the Middle East. The language is used in many magical texts throughout the olden days. Many magical varieties of the tongue are considered to be threatened.

Ancient Aramaic refers to the earliest known period of the language, from its origin until it became the official 'lingua franca' of the Fertile Crescent. You ought to take it upon yourself to study and understand it.

Archaic Egyptian

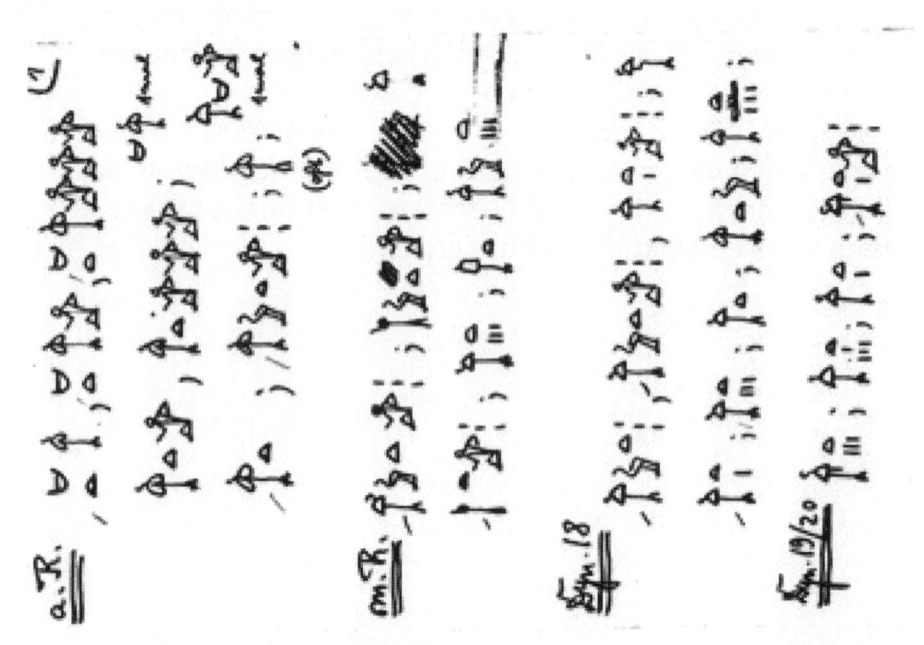

Archaic Egyptian is the mother tongue of Egypt. It is one of the oldest documented languages. Egyptian was uttered until the late 17th century CE in the form of Coptic. A number of Coptic texts were written on various materials, including papyrus, paper, bones and pots, which invoke necromantic and paranormal protections evidently distinguishable as magical.

Ancient Greek

Ancient Greek is the historical stage in the development of the Greek language, spanning across the Archaic, Classical and Hellenistic periods of ancient Greece and the ancient world. It is dated in the second millennium BC by Mycenaean Greek. Its Hellenistic phase is known as Koine ("common") or Biblical Greek, and its late period mutates imperceptibly into Medieval Greek. Koine is regarded as a separate historical stage of its own, although in its earlier form, it closely resembles Classical Greek. Prior to the Koine and earlier periods, classic Greek included several regional dialects.

The Ancient Greek language is one of the most prominent in human, historians, playwrights and philosophers during the Athenian Golden Age, and of the New Testament. It has made a large contribution to the vocabulary of English and was a standard subject of study in Western educational institutions, from the Renaissance to the early 20th century. The New Latin used in the scientific binomial classification system, continues today to draw vigorously from Ancient Greek vocabulary.

Enochian

ϡ A	٦ I	٦ S
ⴸ B	ᴄ L	⁄ T
ᛒ C	ℇ M	ƶ U
ⵎ D	Ↄ N	ƶ V
ᒣ E	Ⳙ O	ƶƶ W
⸻ F	Ω P	Γ X
Ⴆ G	⊔ Q	⁊ Y
☉ H	ℰ R	ⴹ Z

    Enochian is a title often assigned to an occult or angelic tongue recorded in the private journals of Dr. John Dee and his seer Edward Kelley. It was divulged to them by angels, while some present-time scholars of magic claim these 'angels' were, in fact, demons cloaked as angels.

    The angelical language, as communicated to Dee and Kelley, encompasses a limited text corpus. Supplementally, some sections come with English interpretations. Nonetheless, some linguists, notably Donald Laycock, have studied Enochian, arguing against any unusual characteristics in the language.

    Dee's chronicles did not illustrate the language as "Enochian", instead adopting the names: "Angelical", the "Tongue of Angels", or "Adamical" because, according to these Angels, it was used by Adam, in Paradise, to "label" all existing things. The term "Enochian" comes from Dee's declaration that the Biblical Patriarch

Enoch had been the last human to know the language.

In 1581, Dee said that God had sent "pure angels" to divulge directly with prophets. With Kelley's aid as a scryer, Dee set out to introduce long-lasting connection with the angels, which resulted, among other things, in the acceptance of the Enochian language.

According to Dee's records, Angelical was said to be the tongue used by God to design the universe, and which was later used by Adam to speak with God and his angels, and to name all things in existence. After his descend from heaven, Adam lost the language and composed a form of proto-Hebrew based upon his fuzzy recollection of Angelical. This proto-Hebrew was the all embracing human language until the time of the Confusion of Tongues at the Tower of Babel.

From the time of Adam to the time of Dee and Kelley, Angelical was kept hidden from mortals with the unique exception of the father Enoch, who, according to the angels, published the Book of Loagaeth (Speech from God) for humanity. The book was said to be stolen.

The reception of Enochian began on March 26 1583, when Kelley reported apparitions in a crystal, of the twenty-one lettered alphabet characteristic of the language. A few days later, Kelley began absorbing what became the first corpus of texts in the Angelic language. This was reported in the book Liber Loagaeth ("Book of Speech from God").

The book includes the forty-nine "calls" or charms in the Angelic language, but also of ninety-five considerable letter tables, or squares made of forty-nine by forty-nine letters. Dee and Kelly said the angels never bothered interpreting the texts in this book.

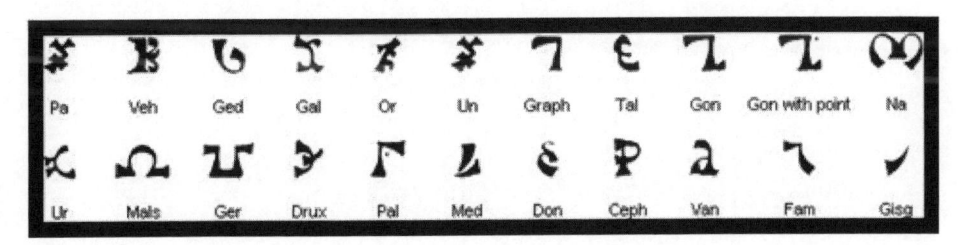

Pa	Veh	Ged	Gal	Or	Un	Graph	Tal	Gon	Gon with point	Na
Ur	Mals	Ger	Drux	Pal	Med	Don	Ceph	Van	Fam	Gisg

Gothic

Gothic is a lost magical tongue that was spoken by the Goths. It is known principally from the Codex Argenteus, and is the only East Germanic language with a sizable corpus.

It is the Germanic language with the earliest attestation, but has no contemporary descendants. The oldest records in Gothic date back to the 4th century. The language was in decrease by the mid-6th century, due to the downfall of the Goths and their exile. The language endured in some parts of modern Spain as late as the 8th century, and Walafrid Strabo wrote that it was still uttered in isolated mountain regions in Crimea in the early 9th century. Gothic-like terms found in later manuscripts might not belong to the same language.

DIVINE LANGUAGE ADAMIC

The Adamic language is the human speech uttered by Adam in the beginning of time. Adamic is also the language used by God to address Adam. There is no documentation of the teaching of this language, so it could be complicated to grasp.

BIBLICAL HEBREW

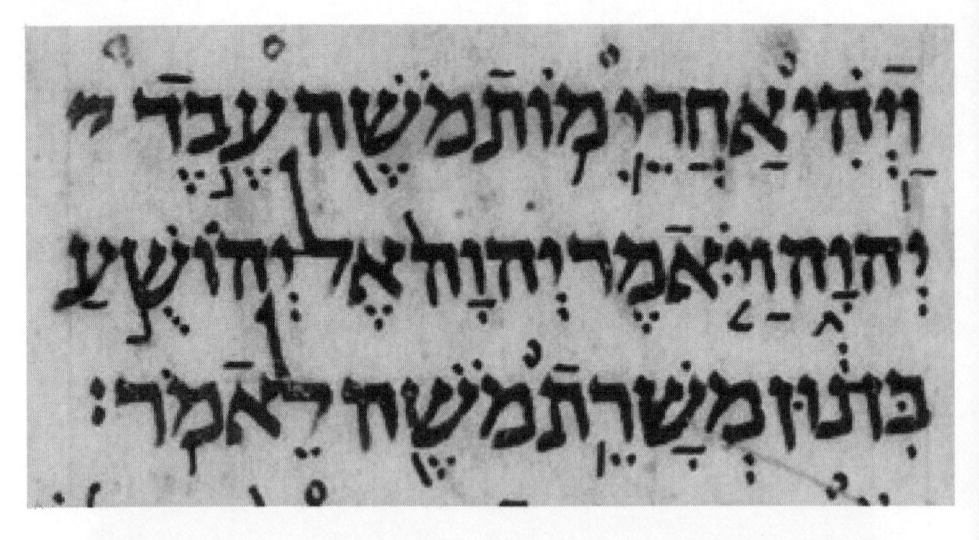

Biblical Hebrew, also called Traditional Hebrew, is the archaic form of the Hebrew tongue in which the Hebrew Bible and various Israelite engravings were written.

It is not uttered in its pure form today, although it is often studied by wizards and witches, to help them gain a greater perception of the many mystic texts found in magical works, such as the Goetia, Book of the Bahir, Harba-De-Moshe, etc.

Biblical Hebrew and present-day Hebrew conflict with respect to grammar, vocabulary, and phonology. Although Modern and scriptural Hebrew's grammatical laws often differ, Biblical Hebrew is occasionally used in Modern Hebrew publications, much as archaic and Biblical constructions are used in Modern English literature.

From the scripts of Osari The Wise
(section 75, page 2)

"Words are authority, the sovereignty of speech is lustier than the power of a thought by itself, for all that thought comes to be manner, upon utterance, you unleash the rule of your purpose, only then – creation begins. When concerning magic, it does not matter what human speech you designate, it is of the utmost significant that the language bestows strengths upon you: you may utter English, Hebrew, or Hellenic – if the language empowers your spirit, the stronger the authority of your magic" – Osari the Wise, 1907.

A Wizard's Mind

*"For everyone who asks receives; he who seeks finds;
And to him who knocks, the door will be opened" - Jesus*

What is My Nature?

When gaining knowledge of magic, one must conclude upon the chief class of magic they wish to attend, such as the convention of nature magic, high magic, necromancy, spell casting, etc. Becoming specialized in one distinct grade of magic will grant you the proficiency you need to practice magic with great meticulousness,

Remember, the more familiar you are, the longer the procedure may take; the magical force of the caster increases with knowledge and relentless 'mana' regeneration.

The notion of 'energy' is set apart for those who wish to obtain 'magical mana' attainable at any given moment. Those who are involved in spirit conjuring do not have to worry about mana and instant power. A spirit conjuration can be accomplished by calling on higher powers to deploy their life-force to do your bidding.

A conjurer is simply an ethereal coordinator, not a true spell caster, and therefore, is not required to 'collect' energy; the same is true for necromancers.

However, if you choose to mature into a necromancer, witch, white magician, or a mage, you will need to meditate daily. Enlightenment is the proper path to rejuvenating mana (magical energy), and only upon enlightenment, will meditation be effective.

Therefore, the first step to becoming enlightened and gathering mana is by performing daily magical meditations.

A Wizard's Guide to Enlightenment

Most of you reading this will have relished enlightenment at one point, without comprehending it. In addition, you will not have grasped it considering that "it" is usually so distinctive from presumptions, you most likely evaded the importance of those moments. You should disregard your current concepts with regard to enlightenment.

The greatest predicament with enlightenment being promoted in the media these days, is the conviction that it is a singular and conclusive state of mind. Therefore, distinct educators bestow contradictory guidance on what it is and how to obtain it.

If we grasp the progression of magical enlightenment, and perhaps its goal, we accept that enlightenment itself is not singular. Much as we comprehend the many paths to God or magic, we can unmask the many paths to enlightenment.

The meaning of magical enlightenment to you will be contingent upon the type of individual you are, and this will determine the path you must take. Here are seven predominant archetypes of established enlightenment in human culture today:

Physical Enlightenment: This class of enlightenment is achieved when we are engrossed in the physicality of our physical bodies; it is distinguished by a tranquil lack of movement and emptiness of mind. It is not to be confused with a materialist perspective. In this class, the physical expression of our being is used as the anchor of our focus. This form of non-mystical experience path is chosen by the stoic Eastern mind. The focus is on improving pure and fundamental consciousness of the physical processes. While physical enlightenment is articulated in Buddhism and yoga, it tends to be pursued in physical activities and exercise regimes. This is the slowest path to enlightenment and can take many years to reach. In fact, because of the fundamental nature of this form, those who achieve physical enlightenment are generally unaware of it.

Intellectual Enlightenment: This form of enlightenment uses intellectual thinking to comprehend the restraints of mind in perceiving what is "reality"; and in doing so, it provokes a freed mind (Similar to the one described in the 'Matrix' films). The mind is used here to exceed the power of one's mind. This type tends to be promoted by gurus who are more self-reliant.

The anchor used here is consciousness, and it is related to physical enlightenment, because, with no mind, consciousness will often fall back onto the physical procedures such as 'the breath.' You will find countless introverts on this path to enlightenment, and it is mostly supported by men. This grade of enlightenment can be achieved quickly if one is focused enough.

Psychological Enlightenment: This class of nirvana use self-analysis, psychoanalysis and the genuine maturing process of the 'self' to reach complete mental fusion, wherein the ego is not blotted out, but integrated. The path tends to attract contemplative people (Such as Freud and Jung).

Religious Enlightenment: This form of enlightenment embraces the love of a God. It is portrayed by human compassion. This path is best for those who emotionally relate to the world, and project what is within out onto others — the path of the extrovert.

Energetic Enlightenment: This grade of nirvana focuses on energy and the understanding of energy in the physical world. It tends to be favored by introverts and is distinguished by prevailing energetic states, psychic or healing powers, obscure knowledge and a powerful influence on others. This is the path of Buddhist tantra and particular forms of tantric yoga, including Kriya yoga. Enlightenment on this path can mature instinctively at any time, or be the result of a lifetime's focus of building the right energetic vehicle.

Shamanic Enlightenment: This grade of enlightenment focuses on the human link to spiritual energy. The shaman has a spiritual bond with the spiritual world — which he uses to affect the physical world and communicate with spiritual beings. Throughout a shaman's life, he or she will develop their relationship with spirits, learning to move through spiritual dimensions and into other worlds with greater ease and eagerness. At first, this is done gradually, only materializing when the shaman goes into a trance, but with years of experience, the shaman becomes more conscious of these other dimensions and spirits in everyday life. Shamanic Enlightenment tends to be handed down from teacher to student, who can introduce the student to the spirits that the teacher has built a relationship with. Shamanism is generally 'attracted' to those who experienced near-death events.

Magical Enlightenment: This grade of enlightenment incorporates a direct mystical unity with the divine — the path of the mystic —where the 'inner' grows into 'the outer' and the outer becomes the inner. It is distinguished by pre-eminent visions, prophecy and supernatural experiences.

Magical Enlightenment is the sparsest and the most unconstrained form. Those who attain it will often experience mystical encounters from early childhood, and it can be the most daunting of the paths, as even fundamental consciousness is not enough to anchor the practitioner during these experiences.

Most tend to develop it instinctively at some point in their lives. Wizards and witches (teachers) tend to be more uncooperative and do not commonly approve of disciples. They tend to be outcasts and loners, often appreciated after death.

What are the magic traits that characterize enlightened states? That truly rests upon your cultural and personal beliefs. These beliefs establish the way you "brand" a state of awareness, and how you brand that state of consciousness will establish your response to it and your conduct within it. It will also determine other people's reaction to you while you are in that state. For example, what may seem as an enlightened state to an Intellectual Enlightenment group, might appear as a compulsive state of awareness from a Psychological Enlightenment group perspective. What is considered enlightenment changes substantially from one person to the other, often leading to over-sensitivity between groups.

Enlightenment is a particular adapted state of awareness, one that "release" us from the mental prison we live in. There are numerous ways of extracting our identity from everyday experience so that we can reach the different types of enlightenment. Anybody who has THE solution, THE state and THE method is just spouting spiritual fundamentalism. The beauty of the spiritual path is that it is often unique for each of us, especially in the West where individuality is more pronounced. This is because the ego plays its part in the enlightening process for Western type minds. It is NOT the bogeyman that needs only to be annihilated. It can be our ally, and we only fool ourselves if we think that the solution to the narcissistic egotism that grips Western society is the annihilation of the ego altogether. Rather, it is the integration of ego so that it plays its proper function. (If you want to see how egoless people function in this world, then you might consider visiting a mental health hospital rather than an ashram.

The fundamental lack of understanding of what enlightenment is the unconsciousness of its abundance, and the narrow mindedness to other spiritual paths and distinctive representation that this ignorance produces. This is why so few understand these enlightened states in their lifetime; the odds are microscopic because so few have the faith to authentically walk the right path.

This is what Carl Jung suggested when he wrote, "Enlightenment is not imagining figures of light but making the darkness conscious." This darkness represents those aspects of ourselves that we are in the dark about because we have not directed the light of our awareness and acceptance in that direction — they are our unconsciousness. Only when we begin to comprehend and integrate all aspects of our being can we understand, let alone walk, our individual path to enlightenment.

When we realize that all this time in spiritual circles, we have been dealing with different states of spiritual consciousness, which we have collectively and confusingly labeled "enlightenment", we start to understand the enormous creativity of the universe and the blessing of our individuality. Moreover, in this realization, we can relax and open-mindedly explore. We begin to realize that life is a creative and explosive venture; we do not return to the source, but the source comes to us as we spiral out into infinity, spinning our creative dreams of ever-greater possibility. (Just stop me any time... I am just expressing my mystical/psychological truth and I am sure you have a different and equally valid truth.

Enlightenment is what you make it. So rather than regard it as an elite spiritual club that divides the enlightened from the unenlightened, throw away your coveted membership application and start honoring the living spirit that is working in your life each moment. Relax and go with the flow, ride life's waves even if you think that in moments, you are being unspiritual and unenlightened. Only when we stop using awful labels like "enlightenment" and "spiritual" can we find the path that we are supposed to take, a path with no destination that is, in itself, a destination. Let go of spiritual fascism and open to a true respect for yourself and your neighbor on this journey towards the infinite.

Therefore, if you still desire the attainment of enlightenment, here is a modest prescription:

1) Disregard the folklore, and realize that it can be manifested in different ways depending upon your individuality, beliefs, culture, and the form of magic you wish to practice; there are no requirements or guidelines.

2) Discover which distinct form of enlightenment suits you the best. Traditionally, it will be a combination of paths; when in doubt, debate it with a confidante who knows you very well.

3) If you feel the urge to pursue enlightenment, you should direct your utter care towards it. You should also remember, as you develop along the path you adopt, the aim will reform as you develop. You may surrender your quest altogether if your apprehension of enlightenment no longer holds the same appeal to you.

4) Study the subsequent chapter in this book titled 'Reaching Enlightenment'. This chapter addresses the procedures needed to accomplish your aim.

Mind and Energy

Wizards understand that the universe, nature and divine nature are the same. Divinity is fundamental in Nature, and divinity is inherently evident in every living and spiritual being and thing. Therefore, we feel the pervasive deity in Nature and within ourselves. We know that the realm of Nature is comprised of the physical world (Earth) as well as the spiritual world (Divine).

Therefore, even though we speak of god and goddess, and may refer to them with the archaic titles by which they are known; we see them as embodiments of the divine. They convey the intangible notion of pantheism in a way that can be understood. Thus, the Horned God who was consequential to our genetic past is the embodiment of the male 'ingredient' of Nature, as is the Goddess of the Moon, the embodiment of the female regenerative aspect of Nature.

Pantheism conceives the fact that "Energy is all" and "All is energy." Pantheism helps witches and wizards see the world as it really is: energy.

We are all an undivided section of energy (God). I am God; you are God; the book you are reading is God; everything that "exists" in the world is God. In short, everything in the perfect cosmos is one essence, and that essence is Energy. We all live in the same divine plane. We are not "separate" from others, from our environment, nor from God. We do not think separate thoughts, feel separate feelings, nor make separate choices. As we mentioned before, you could see it as living inside a 'computer software,' powered by the energy that is God.

"Everything I have accepted up to now as being absolutely true and assured, I have learned from or through the senses. But I have sometimes found that these senses played me false it is prudent never to trust entirely those who have once deceived us...Thus what I thought I had seen with my eyes, I actually grasped solely with the faculty of judgment, which is in my mind"

The Law of Magic

Every section of the human body vibrates energy. Your brain has a singular set of brain-waves. In neuroscience, there are a five separate wave frequencies: Beta, Alpha, Theta, Delta and the humble 'Gamma.' Understanding and developing your wizard's mind at the greater states of awareness will open your eyes to the nature of your repressed mind and higher-self where you can begin to use magic and influence "reality" at will. Each frequency, calculated in "cycles per second" (Hz), has its individual set of attributes symbolizing a fixed level of mind activity and hence a state of consciousness, which will give you the power to practice magic.

The average individual has between 10,000 and 45,000 thoughts a day. This suggests that your aim should be to control your mind before you can practice the craft. If you permit negative thoughts to penetrate your mind, your magical creations will fail.

It is your influential thoughts and beliefs that you must learn to bear under your self-conscious authority, as they are what largely conclude your ability to perform magic. As you do, you will begin to experience the powers of thought.

The confidential secret of magical demonstration is that you "attract" your cravings by what your mind conceives and what your body feels. If you beckon a spell upon an individual, your intellect and sensations must be in complete union. Everything is God (energy), and you create magic by utilizing your mind and body to influence the physical world.

It is your feelings and thoughts that influence magic. The more you experience the feeling of obtaining a specific result in a magic procedure or spell, the stronger the effect will be. Higher vibrations and sensations will create stronger magic. This is the law of magic, and if you remember one thing, you must memorize this. The more powerful your thoughts and mental sensations are, the easier it will be to create magic, since magic is energy, and energy is everything. You must understand this concept.

If you live in energy, breath energy and think energy, you are influencing energy.

Strong feelings and powerful thoughts will help you influence reality. When you truly believe in magic, love and cherish it, you can produce it more independently. You have the authority to manifest energy (magic) and anything else you might want to attract in life! Whatever you turn your attention (focus) to, you will create. As a wizard, you should accept the definite truth. "The Law of Attraction" is a considerable example of these lessons. Individuals who set free their minds from the unseen prison are then able to affect their environment by offering different thoughts.

Achieving Enlightenment

Most wizards support the use of meditation to reach enlightenment. Each magician has their own process of meditation but underlying them is consequential. This point is linked to the way you restrain your concentration. If you can keep your concentration unquestionably still, not letting it wander about as it usually does, and keeping it completely fixed upon the meditation object you have chosen, you will sustain the most overwhelming mental states you will ever experience. This is no easy task. Witches, wizards and even monks spend hours, days, months and even years in meditation to achieve it. Once this fixation has been attained, you should observe the following:

1) Your thought process will cease. If you are unable to sustain your focus, your thought process will kick in again, and you will come back to your habitual state.

2) You will focus and merge into the current moment and experience universal awareness.

3) Time will halt. You will be aware only of the "immediate moment." Past and future will discontinue, since they are concepts of your thought process.

4) Your 'self' will vanish. Since your ego is only a complicated form of concepts and thoughts, it will fade as soon as your thought process halt. You might think that this would be a frightening experience. However, it is the contrary. As soon as your thought process rests, there is a vast sense of easement and mental liberty.

5) You will feel the company of magnificent bliss. 'Bliss' is the instinctive state of the soul, which we rarely experience because we are so concerned and captivated with our daily thought process and the "outer universe."

6) You will experience other marvelous and unfamiliar feelings, and you will come to fathom that "you" are just a state of awareness. Everything else, including the earth, our flesh, our mind, our sensations, feelings, emotions and thoughts are repeatedly changing and ultimately vanish. Our awareness doesn't shift and is always present. Our awareness is limitless. It is our connection to the Divine. We use our mind to create this awareness.

    We are energy and therefore, we are boundless and an essential function of God. No matter how demanding magic may be for you, you should not dwell upon it. You may conceive the notion that a particular spell will not work or be effective, and therefore, it will not be effective. The slightest negative thought in your practice will result in failure. Trade with these thoughts the best way you can; in other words, control your mind. Experiment the following: Meditate before a mental image and keep your mind pure of any other image for at least two hours, during these two hours, you must prevent any other thought from penetrating your mind.

Success in this experiment will result in utter control over your thoughts. But do not force it, you should let your higher-self be the concluding guide and know that the complete path takes place inside your awareness.

Meditation

Ultimately, you will be able to endure magical thoughts at all times, even in the most unmanageable conditions. The aim of meditation is to keep our minds still and tranquil. If our intellect is still, you will be liberated from concerns and mental faze.

In addition, we will be able to exercise magic without the weight of defeatism or mistrust that we are doing wrong; if your mind is not peaceful, you will find it remarkably unmanageable to use magic, regardless of knowledge. If we come to be skillful "meditators", our minds will progressively become more serene, and we will be able to carry out mightier grades of magic.

Unenlightened mortals find it difficult to command their minds. It appears as if their minds are in control of their thoughts – not the other way around. If their experience in the world is positive, their mind thinks positive thoughts, but if it is negative, they immediately become negative minded. For example, if we are trying to carry out a spell or other magical act, and it fails, we will possibly become irritated and feel distressed with the consequence that we failed to achieve and will feel as if it is all pointless.

By training in meditation, we establish an innerspace and lucidity that authorize us to control our minds; such shifts of mood arise because we are too concerned in the superficial situation. We can learn to control our minds regardless of the superficial occurrences. Gradually, we develop balance, a stable mind that is joyful and sympathetic all the time, rather than an unstable mind that wobbles between the extremes of joy and discouragement.

If we train in meditation methodically, we will be able to annihilate the deceptions that are the sources of all our difficulties and pain. In this way, we will come to experience an imperishable inner peace, known as nirvana. Then, we will experience peace and happiness, and since we know that our thoughts affect our 'reality,' when we are convinced in our powers to execute magic, we will not attract failure.

Breathing Meditations

In general, the objective of breathing meditation is to relax the mind and improve upon inner peace. We can use this form of meditations exclusively or as an introductory routine to diminish our distractions, before dealing with magical meditation.

A Simple Breathing Meditation

The first phase of meditation is to hinder diversions and make our minds clear and pure. This is mastered by carrying out a simple routine. We find a peaceful place to meditate and sit in a relaxed physical position. We can sit in the conventional 'cross-legged posture' or in any other comfortable pose. If we wish, we can sit on the grass or in a chair. The most consequential thing is to maintain a straight back to prevent our minds from becoming lethargic or drowsy.

Osari the Wise advises meditating on a high plane; if you live in the city, it may be a rooftop, or a mountaintop in nature. This helps you to better unite with the divine, since there are no disturbances around.

We sit with our eyes slightly shut and focus on breathing. We breathe naturally, preferentially through the nostrils, without aiming to restrain our breath, and we try to grow conscious of the physical 'sensation' we experience when we breathe in and out. This sensation is our purpose of this meditation.

At first, our minds will be occupied with other matters, and we might even feel that the meditation is provoking a disordered mind, we are becoming more conscious of how occupied our minds really are. There will be a considerable lure to focus upon the distinctive thoughts as they arise, but we should keep our mind exclusively focused upon the sensation of breath. If we uncover that our minds have drifted and are unable to focus upon our breath, we should be consciously attentive and immediately change our focus to the breath. We should repeat this as many times as needed until the mind becomes fixated on the breath for the rest of the session.

Osari the wise, advocates focusing upon our Nefesh (Spirit); as mentioned in the "Soul" chapter. The Nefesh is the spirit present within your "Avatar." Shut your eyes and ponder: The avatar (your physical 'self') is managed by your Nephesh, located in a divine plane.

If we practice tolerantly in this way, our occupying thoughts will progressively diminish, and we will perceive a sense of inner-tranquility, relaxation and enjoyment, Our minds will feel clear and spacious, and we will feel reinvigorated. When the never-ending flow of our disturbing thoughts is quietened through concentration, our minds become exceptionally clear and we will be able to stay with this phase of mental peace for prolonged periods of time.

Even though breathing meditation is only an introductory to magical meditation, it can be quite overwhelming. This form of meditation will help us experience inner peace and serenity just by commanding the mind, without having to rely upon external conditions. So much of the strain and anxiety we generally experience come from within. When the turmoil of occupying thoughts diminishes and our minds become calm, a profound sense of serenity spontaneously arises from within. This feeling of magical peace helps us manage our hectic mind. Just by practicing breathing meditation for thirty minutes each day for thirty days, we will be able to grow into enlightened beings.

We will experience a serene feeling in the mind, and many of our negative thoughts will diminish. Practicing elaborate magic ceremonies will invite gloomy thoughts to any newcomer. Your life will become easier, and magic will be drawn to you as your confidence evolves. Meditation keeps the mind pure and will become a daily ritual for the enlightened wizards. Magic requires the complete command of the mind, and so you must exercise your mind through meditation.

Magical Meditation

Even necromancers have care and respect for all living things, in fact – practitioners of all forms of magic understand and appreciate the power of enlightenment.

What is the goal of meditation?

Through meditation, we will be able to focus upon our magical objectives, and will be able to reach greater levels of realization. The chief aim of all Magical meditations is to direct our mind towards the path to nirvana by attracting the deepest levels of realization.

When a druid accomplished a flawless state of concern towards the wild, he will never again be capable of willingly inflicting harm upon any living thing; all of our subsequent conducts are guided by compassion towards them, so we grow into genuine druids. When a necromancer attained a perfect realization of compassion towards the suffering of the dead and the authorities of the living, they gain more respect towards them, and carry out necromancy with greater sentimental force.

When a witch gains a pure understanding of love and compassion towards plants and herbs, she will always treat them with the utmost reverence, which will bring about fiercer forms of herb magic.

How to Meditate

Magical meditation attracts a magical state of mind and will lead to magical enlightenment. There are five essential stages to successful magical meditation:

1) **Foundation**
2) **Reflection**
3) **Meditation**
4) **Devotion**
5) **Practice**

The 'foundation' incorporates the preliminaries for successful meditation by purifying limitations generated by our past negative actions, empowering our mind with merit, and uplifting it with the invocations of divine spirits. Our meditation custom will be successful if we prepare ourselves carefully.

Much like the process of planting seeds, we must first remove any object that could hinder their growth above the soil, such as rocks and weeds. Second, we enrich the soil with fertilizer to give it the strength to nourish growth. Then, we must provide warm, moist conditions to allow the seeds to sprout and the plants to grow. In the same way, to nurture our inner crops of supernatural realizations, we must begin by meticulously planning. First, we must cleanse our mind to eradicate negative karma, because if we do not purify our mind it will hinder the development of magical realizations. Second, we need to give our mind the force to reinforce the growth of magical realizations by accumulating merit. Third, we need to activate and nourish the growth of magical realizations by connecting our mind with the divine.

There are three mandatory foundations for successful meditation: cleansing negativity, accumulating merit, and connecting our mind with the divine.

It is very important to unite with the divine. As we acknowledged earlier, upon executing advanced forms magic we are tapping into the existence of God itself, and are utilizing the privileges with which we were glorified with.

Receiving blessings from the divine is influential, and it adapts our mind by initiating our high-minded abilities, nourishing the growth of our magical realizations, and carrying our magical practices to fruition, think about this – how well might you execute magic, if you know that you had God's approval?

Prayers for Meditation

You may embark on these preliminary procedures by repeating the following charms, while contemplating their meaning:

All is Energy

(We visualize ourselves and all other living beings in their Nephesh state, see them as the energy source they are):

> "God is energy and I am God; the world is God and every living or dead thing on this earth, is a part of the same energy source."

Blessing of the Wizard

> "Through the use of source energy and my link to the divine world, I shall be able to use the forces bestowed upon me by the divine world. I will now grow into a Wizard for the good of all living or dead things." (3x)

Generating the four immeasurable:

> "I ask God, the source of energy force,
> To grant me the force,
> May I receive his grace,
> To act, accomplish and produce new magic,
> For the benefit of all the living and the dead,
> May God grant me his blessing, and I shall be his agent upon this earth."

Visualizing

> "In the space before me is the living God surrounded,
> By all the wizards and the witches, like the full moon surrounded by stars."

Prayer of Necromancers

"Oh, noblest Source Energy! I say thou art welcome unto me, I shall call upon your angels and demons, the spirits of the dead and the spirits of the living - through you, who has created the earth, and the divine, and the never-ending plane of energy, and all that is in them contained.
Give me the strengths to summon the dead.
Give me the strengths to speak, to ask and to see.
Give me your blessing to practice under your name and command.

Prayer of White Wizards

The ground sprinkled with perfume and spread with flowers. The Great Mountain, four lands, sun and moon.

"Oh, noblest Source Energy! I say thou art welcome unto me, I shall use your energies of good and heal through you, who have created all dead and living things.
Give me the power to heal the ill, to console the grieving.
Give me the force to create pure Kesem, to shape illusions and command good angles.
Give me your blessing to practice under your name and command.
Release me from the prison of evil deeds and dark Kesheph."

Prayer of Druids

Thank you for the charming land you have given to the trees, the plants and us;
The animals and the insects, the flowers and mountains and all things that are nature.
I am one with nature; I am one with the trees; I am one with all living creatures.
I am the son/daughter of the forest, and is one with it.
Give me the force to heal the ill, to utter the tongue of beasts, to command nature and the forces of the wild.
Give me the strength to compose Kesem, to speak to the bird, and the snake and the butterfly.
Give me your blessing to practice under your name and your command.
Give me the power of nature; give me the power of the forest.

(1) Foundation (1)

By the virtues I have collected,
By practicing the stages of the path,
May all living beings find the chance
To practice in the same way.
May I attain magical enlightenment,
Give me the power of _____, and let me harvest it under your command.

(2) Reflection (2)

The intention of reflection is to bring to mind the purpose of magical meditation. We do this by considering various lines of reasoning, contemplating metaphors, and reflecting upon the scriptures. It is beneficial to remember the examinations given in each section so that we can meditate without looking for mention in the text. The contemplations given here are intended only as guidelines.

(3) Meditation (3)

When, through our reflections, our magical aim appears clearly in our mind, we focus on the object exclusively.

When we begin to meditate, our mind is cluttered; we are effortlessly diverted and frequently lose our focus. If we desire to practice necromancy we will meditate and focus on compassion towards the dead, we begin by contemplating the agony experienced by the dead upon their passing, until a strong feeling of connection arises in our heart. When this feeling arises, we meditate on it single-mindedly. If the feeling fades, or if our mind drifts, we should force our focus upon the result.

Magical meditation familiarizes our mind with magical objects. The more familiar we are with such objects, the more peaceful our mind becomes. By training in meditation, and living in accordance with the comprehensions developed during meditation, ultimately we shall be able to retain a magical mind continuously throughout our life.

(4) Devotion (4)

Devotion guides the mana provoked by our meditation towards the realization of magical enlightenment. By repeating the previous chants genuinely at the end of each meditation session, we guarantee that the mana we produced by meditating is not wasted, but acts as a cause for enlightenment; in addition, we ensure that our mind is at ease and in full connection with the divine.

(5) Practice (5)

This consists of suggestion on how to integrate magical meditation into our daily life. It is significant to retain that magical practice is not constricted to our occupations during the meditation session; it should fill our entire life. We should not permit a void between meditation, because the attainment of our meditation pivots upon the purity of our conduct outside the meditation session. We should be conscious of our thoughts at all times by applying heedfulness, alertness, and conscientiousness; and we should try to abandon whatever bad habits we may have. Deep experience of magic is the result of skilled training over a long period of time, especially during magic; therefore, we should practice steadily and smoothly, without being in a hurry to see results. So

Magical commands are not given purely for the sake of academic understanding of the path to enlightenment. They are granted to obtain deep magical experience, and should therefore be put into practice. If we train our mind in these meditations every day, we will soon gain pure realizations of all the stages of the path. Until we have attained this stage, we should not tire of listening to oral teachings on magic, or reading about our selected path of magic (whether it's necromancy or druidism), and contemplate and meditate on these instructions. We need to expand our understanding of these fundamental topics, and to use this new understanding to improve our other forms of meditation.

From the scripts of Osari The Wise
(section 1, page 8)

"The existence was composed of thought; when God created the cosmos, he composed it with his thought, and when a thought enters time and space, it initiates the practice of making. We coin the world around us by thoughts and ways; wizards create magic by using thought and intelligent ways as well, and we are who we think we are..." – Osari the Wise, 1907.

The Wizard's Posture

When we practice magical meditation, we need to sit in a relaxed posture. It is a good idea to become familiar with the monk posture. If we cannot hold this posture, we should sit on a cushion, which is as close as possible while remaining comfortable. The seven characteristics of the wizard's posture are similar to those of Buddhists:

(1) The legs are crossed in the vajra posture.

(2) The right hand is located in the left hand palms upwards, with the tips of the thumbs partly raised and gently touching. The hands are held about four fingers' width below the navel. This helps us to evolve good concentration. The right hand symbolizes 'creativity' and the left hand symbolizes 'wisdom' – the two together symbolize the unity of creativity and wisdom. The two thumbs at the level of the navel symbolize the blazing of creative creation.

(3) The back is upright, but not tense. This helps us to enhance and maintain a clear mind, and it permits the profound energy winds to flow freely.

(4) Your lips and teeth should be relaxed, but the tongue touches against the back of the upper teeth. This heads off excessive salivation, while also stopping our mouth from becoming too dry.

(5) The head is leaning forward, with the chin tucked in so that the eyes are cast down. This helps avert mental exhilaration.

(6) The eyes are utterly closed; this will remove any visual distractions.

(7) The shoulders are level, and the elbows are held slightly away from the sides to let air circulate.

If we want to begin generating mana, we need to clear away all our negative thoughts and distractions. A further characteristic of magical posture is the preparatory breathing meditation, which increases the accuracy and intensity of our brain waves. This directs our focus upon a specific magical aim and brings-forth results in magic. However, when we first meditate, our minds are usually crowded with disquieting thoughts, and cannot immediately convert back to the virtuous state we need as our motivation. We can accomplish this by practicing breathing meditation.

Breathing Meditation

When we sit comfortably on our meditation seat, we begin by becoming aware of the thoughts that are passing through our minds. Then we slowly turn our notice to our breath, letting its tempo remain normal. As we breathe out, we visualize that we are exhaling all distressing and negative thoughts, in the form of black smoke that fades into space. As we inhale, we visualize that we are inhaling all the invocations and imagination of the holy beings, in the form of white light that comes into our body and fills up our heart. We nourish this visualization exclusively with each inhalation and exhalation for one hour or until our mind has become calm and attentive. If we concentrate on our breathing in this way, negative thoughts and distractions will temporarily disappear, because we cannot concentrate on more than one object at a time.

Using Speech to Invoke Magic

Every country in the world has its own set of Mantras. As spoken thoughts, Mantras have always been used to heal, to protect, to attract love, to attract wealth and are an important part of magic, spells and wizardry.

In the past, marching armies would chant or sing mantras before going into combat for the sake of inspiring their fellow noblemen. Vikings used to chant 'Odin, Odin, Odin' as they charged towards their enemies. It is said that the power of Odin's chant provoked the enemy to break and run.

The archaic Egyptians used to chant the names of great demons while demonstrating their powers to Moses, who arrived to release the Israelites. A Mantra, be it a mental intonation, a chant or a full-blown shout, is all about energy. Mantras get their powerful vibrations from the Energy Source, or as some call it, "The Mind of God." The science behind Energy Source is called the Laws of Quantum Physics.

A wizard knows that there is no time, no past, present nor future in energy. There is no space, nor distance. Only the here, only the now! The Energy Source responds to our thoughts. Our words are a form of spoken thoughts, and they have the capacity to influence energy; we do this by generating brain waves. Remember the phrase: "Our thoughts create our physical reality."

The spoken word is uttered by our mouth, but the force behind it is coming from our mind. Our brain-waves emit focused energy and when you speak with emotion you focus that energy out into the atmosphere.

(1) "I am an energy being dwelling in the light surrounded and carried by spiritual powers."

(2) "I dwell in perfect peace profound, my kingdom now is here and found."

(3) "God Guides
God Provides
God Heals
God Reveals
God Protects
God Perfects."

Visualize

Visualization is a procedure used by wizards to 'transfer' energy manipulation (magic) from the creativity (the mind) to the physical world. During your magic practice, spell or ritual, you should put your creative mind to work. You should be able to see the magical result manifesting in front of you. The only limit is your own mind.

Visualize the spell, ritual or magical result desired. Know that what you see in your mind is being transformed into reality by use of radio-waves. During a Goetia ritual, for example, you should visualize the demon manifest. 'Daydream' it, work it through your mind and let it grow into existence by use of mental-pictures.

Shift your vision into the physical world. When visualizing, direct your complete focus upon the desired result. Before embarking upon the spell or magic ritual, focus clearly on the 'mental photo' of the magical act you are about to attain. For example, while you are performing a love spell, watch your subject as they fall in love, fantasize about you and increase their desire towards you (in any fashion you wish to visualize it). You are directing your brain-waves to produce this result, and it manifest in the physical world.

Enlightened wizards have the inherent power to produce physical results by use of their mind. Skeptics, however, will neutralize your endeavors and defeat the effectiveness of your visualization session.

CHAPTER 3
ACT

PRACTICING WITCHCRAFT

So, you wish to heal the sick, converse with the natural world, use herbs, cast spells and observe the many forces of nature magic? What follows are some easy-to-understand guidelines for newcomers:

> Step 1: Take it upon yourself to study the many distinctive forms of magic; African Voodoo, Wicca, Hermetic or Ceremonial. They might have numerous similarities, but they are not all identical; therefore, you must select the specific grades of magic you wish to practice.

Step 2: Read as much as you can. After studying the records presented in the previous chapters, you will spend hours in research. There is a lot of intelligence to adopt and this is the most proficient path to obtain it. Make sure you practice formulating spells, potions and magical artifacts.

Step 3: Seek out the guidance of a proficient practitioner. Nothing is more valuable than the wisdom passed down from a high-rank guide. You should never pay for such service! A real witch or wizard will never charge you a penny, but will serve as a mentor.

Step 4: Acknowledge that nature is divine and controls many awe-inspiring secrets. Respect nature, as it is a dominant force in our physical world; meditate one or two hours each day as presented in earlier chapters.

Step 5: Learn to utilize the energy of plants and herbs; learn the appropriate use and energetic qualities of each herb. For a long time, the creative use of herbs was banned on account of the many "terrors of witchcraft...". As you research theory and practice you will rediscover the effects of certain plants on human body and energy.

Step 6: Study the contemporary systems of "Law-of-Attraction" and "Quantum Physics." Although oversimplified at times, the theories described in these laws are based on "science" and tend to illustrate Energy-Source in a way that many people find 'easy to understand'.

Step 7: Practice, practice, practice. Do not miss a single opportunity to practice magic and evaluate the results at the end of each session. You should not yearn for "overnight results." Remember that the proper use of magic takes time and plenty of practice.

Visit metaphysical bookstores and magic shops. These shops tend to carry mystical items such as wands, runes, ritual robes, calendars (showing moon phases, Sabbats, and Esbats), and books on the topic of magic.

Search online for local pagan events open to the public, such as festivals or holiday rituals. These will most likely take place in natural outdoor settings, so dress accordingly. Utilize the meditation techniques presented in the previous chapters. Look within yourself and comprehend your own power. Study the pantheons of distinctive pagan religions (Greek, Roman, Norse, Celtic, etc.) and see which deities speak the most to you. They could be useful to you.

Totem animals may be especially helpful in guidance along with other spirit-guides, contact your Totem animal and build the bond to develop your psychic strength.

WARNING!

- There are still those who will hunt individuals who claim to deal with witchcraft. Remember that it is against the law in some countries to practice any form of magic. Use extreme care around negative and skeptic people.

- Cursing people or casting malevolent charms could have some harmful effects that may possess you; demons and angels do not welcome the invocations of the living.

- Do not try conversing with spirits or demons without knowledge. Make sure you are adept with All the steps needed before undertaking such crafts; follow the books and the steps mentioned in it carefully.

- Do not attempt to practice any forms of magic unless you are enlightened, you will provoke miserable results at best. Complete the steps in this book before deciding to move forward!

Practicing Necromancy

Necromancy became connected with dark magic and demon-summoning in general, occasionally losing its specialized meaning. The most conventional application is evocation a spirit to deliver knowledge from the divine. More extreme applications will attempt the beckoning of dead spirits. You can recover this knowledge in the "Sefer Yetzirah," which is referred to in this book. *The Lesser Keys Of The King Solomon* also contain precise commands for the beckoning of demons and angels.

Necromancy is best accomplished night. Calling upon spirits for the sake of personal gain is a strenuous experience. Demons and angels will always defy the necromancer's efforts to extract information. Therefore, the necromancer must be able to control it.

Influential necromancers can mandate their personal will upon the breathing as well. During the first weeks, you will experience injurious or disturbing dreams, and abnormal episodes from powerful spirits. Try to avoid dealing with demons or spirits you do not know.

Unlike human spirits, angels and demons are disobedient and revengeful. Avoid the summoning of archangels or God itself at all costs, this can lead to death or psychotic hospitalization. You can look for necromantic rituals and spells in the books acknowledged. For genuine results, you should only practice the craft after obtaining enlightenment. Skipping steps will produce disappointment.

Necromantic rituals make use of the remaining energy of dead spirits. You can meditate in a graveyard, under the stars, and accumulate mana before embarking on the ritual or utter the spell. Remember, you must not be timid. Spirits, demons and angels are not "friendly" or behave pleasingly in the company of men. Mental durability and a hardened state-of-mind is needed.

Meditation should last for two-hours, from Midnight to 2AM. The longer the meditation, the easier it will be to contact the spirits. You will endure subtle forms of retaliations and haunting once the meditation is finished.

As you gain experience, you will be able to govern your energy toward nature rather than the spirit plane. Your chances of attainment are lesser since nature spirits are less likely to retort.

Necromantic practice is neither the 'pure' nor the 'evil' path. It is merely a keen attunement to "death energy," the remaining energy left upon the earth after the passing of a human being or beast. However, you must know that the "wisdom" of dead spirits is not unlimited, shades (ghosts) only know certain things. The clear value of their counsel is the result of things they had known in life, or of knowledge they acquired after death. Some necromancers also deal with "bone-conjuring", some deal exclusively with "demon-summoning", or divinations.

The Steps

Note: You will find it easier to practice necromancy when you are in the company of death itself, if you experienced a life-threatening experience in the past, necromantic rituals will appear easier.

Step 1: You must unite with death energy and the agents of death. Spend two hours in a burial ground, or elevated plane where you can serenely meditate. During the meditation, you will spark a bond with "death energy" and endure the agony of the living, who grief for those who passed.

Step 2: Study the art of self-hypnosis, which is perfectly safe. Use this form of hypnosis to obtain trance-like state and find the unconscious origin of knowledge. You can practice self-hypnosis throughout your daily meditation process.

Step 3: You should have an objective in mind; you should realize the "End Goal" of your craft. Make a list of desired books and texts and take it upon yourself to study them.

Step 4: Learn to communicate with the dead by using the meditation and studying the various books mentioned in this book. Start by reading the book 'Goetia,' and 'The Lesser Keys of Solomon'; beckon the fainter demons described in it, and after you have successfully manifested your first demon, you may proceed to summon stronger demons, spirits and angels.

WARNING!

- Do not abuse necromancy. Summoning a spirit to obtain a wicked deed could bring harm upon you, and the spirit you summon may exploit you. Taking this process lightly may result in a Dybbuk, so be warned.

- Beginners will endure nightmares, unfamiliar emotions, daydreams and ghost sightings. Do not practice necromancy if you fear death. As soon as you enter their domain, you will begin to see them and hear them; and unless you are enlightened, completed the earlier steps in this book; this could bring about irreversible psychological damage.

- Be careful! Dealing with necromancy will attract necromantic features, you should be prepared to converse with the dead, prepare to see them, speak with them, and deal with them. Once you walk this path, you cannot turn back; you will begin to see the spirits of the dead, even if you do not wish to. You become a 'medium' for those who perished, and this "gift" cannot be easily dismissed.

- Be respectful to the dead. Be sure to meditate exactly as shown in previous chapters. And remember - never leave the safety of the circle, or remove the protecting ring.

Practicing Druidism

Although antediluvian spiritual practices of Celtic Druidism have left the modern world with very little confirmable history, these enchanting conventions have, nonetheless, became the base for many present-time endeavors at "renewing" the religion. Druidism is a varied tradition, but one that can grant you with a profoundly enjoyable divine experience for those searching for an unconventional, mystic, nature-religion. Though the paths to druidism are far from common. Druid Magic is a spiritual link to nature and the deities which exist in nature. The Druids would call upon the service of the Gods and give an offering to the Gods in return.

Step 1: Connect with nature. Meditate for one hour every day in a completely natural environment; meditating in nature will help you connect with it. Attempt to communicate with distinctive animals, birds, insects, and wild-life, connect with the trees and the glamour of nature persistently.

Step 2: Meditate, meditate, meditate! Get into a state of trance, in which you will be able to converse with nature; try heeding and speaking with nature, try being one with all living beings (although I will not advocate it, some people choose to use LSD and hallucinogenic drugs since they believe it opens the mind and eases the connection).

Step 3: Study herbology and adopt the utilization of herbal energy; learn the appropriate use and energetic qualities of each herb.

Step 4: Create a nature spell book, keep track of the different effects of each plant and its magical qualities. Develop and practice nature-spells, healing, herb-based-ceremonies and the purification of water.

Step 5: Visit Stonehenge: A great way to build a connection with the Druid faith will be to visit Stonehenge in England, the ruins of a great stone obelisk built in ancient times. It is considered by most Druids to be a source of celebrated spiritual power and has played a prominent role in the evolvement of modern Druidism.

Step 6: Follow a path to priesthood with an established order, or start your own order with your personal prerequisites for the position. Druidism is structured with varying, newly created conventions which priesthood preparations you choose to undergo is contingent upon which Druid groups you wish to be associated with. You can find the prerequisites for priesthood and study on the websites of many orders, though you may find that your research leads you to your own conclusions about the requirements of Druidic priesthood.

Magical Elements of Druidisms:

- Aisling- a vision, dream, or possibly an altered state of consciousness.

- Imbas- poetic and divine inspiration, the "fire in the head"; also, possibly refers to a type of altered state of consciousness.

- Immram- journey to the realm of the Gods by a type of "astral" travel. Immram means "sea journey" and it is said that the islands of paradise in the Otherworld exist in the western seas.

- Echtra- this means "adventures" and journeys on holy grounds. This is the type of magic that was experienced by warriors and hunters and those who travelled in the wilderness.
- Fi/rinne- means truth and justice (in one word). This is the binding force, or the way of nature.

- Dra/iocht- this was a word for magic. The literal translation is "what druids do."

Practicing Magic

Magic is the manipulation of energy, clean and simple. Here we will 'simplify' the understanding of energy manipulation, or "magic" and present before you the ten steps to becoming a real wizard, witch or necromancer:

Step 1: Decide upon the leading grade of magic you wish to practice. The "leading" grade of magic speaks of the form of magic you spend the greater part of your time in, your 'expertise'. You can be a necromancer and yet have comprehension and understanding of herbal magic; a witch can still practice different forms of Druidic magic. Magic is non-exclusive. However, if you wish to produce results, you need to focus upon a primary form of magic. You may practice Alchemy, Black Magic, Asatru Magic, Druidic, Nature Magic, Chaos Magic, Ceremonial, Necromancy, Hoodoo, Hermeticism, etc.

Step 2: Reach enlightenment. Spend one or two hours each day in breathing meditation, leading to magical meditation. Seek and peruse enlightenment every day until you find it. Study the different books and texts discussing the subjects of enlightenment. Read the book "The Heart of the Buddha's Teaching" by Thich Nhat Hanh, and "Way of the Wizard," by Deepak Chopra. Buddhism books and techniques will help you reach this goal faster.

Step 3: Read, read, read: Read everything you can about your preferred topic. Read scholarly books, history books, grimoires, library books and sacred texts. Real wizards spend 60% of their time in search of knowledge and practicing that knowledge is essential.

Step 4: Learn to manipulate energy. Use the meditation techniques mentioned in this book to train the mind and manipulate energy, depending on the grade of magic you choose to practice.

Step 5: Join a coven, group or order. If you choose to look for a coven or other pagan group, check out: meetup.com or How-to-become-a-wizard.com. Find a group of like-minded people who want to share their knowledge and traditions with you, do not pay for such a service.

Step 6: Write a wizard's grimoire. Your grimoire is where you ought to document your experiences with magic, demons, spirits, angels. spells and interpretations of magick.

Step 7: Dabble in alchemy. Magicians show natural interest with nature, energy and the forces of mind and matter. Studying Alchemy is a lifetime commitment and every wizard, witch or necromancer should study, and practice it.

Step 8: Sharpen your mind. Wizards are known as "wisemen". You cannot underestimate the power of intelligence. Intelligent folk are systematized and constantly exercise what they've learned.

Step 9: Develop intuition: Wizards have the ability to sense things before anyone else does. You can develop the ability to "see" things before they actually happen. This is matured with the development of 'confidence'. If you state, with power and confidence that something is going to happen - it will. Try it right now: state, visualize and believe that something (could be something small and meaningless) is going to happen, and with the right focus - it will.

Step 10:Visualize. They key to success in any magical endeavor is the use of visualization. Practice and improve upon your visualization skills, as described in the previous chapter.

Just as any other trade, pagan groups and magical orders could include a few scammers, go with your gut when searching for a group. Do not feel persuaded to do anything you feel uneasy with. Read the books acknowledged in the 'reading material' section and achieve nirvana before engaging in practice.

CREATING MAGICAL OBJECTS

A magic item is any object that has magical mana inherent in it. These may act on their own, or be the instruments of the wizard using the,; Magic items comprise a component of Source Energy, meaning that you should commit yourself to produce authoritative mana in Magical meditation. Therefore, you must not skip the earlier steps before proceeding.

Your magic items will generally act as a 'device' to grant you access to supplemental magical abilities. They may give you magical abilities if you lack them, and save you the time required by magical meditation. These items may heighten your energy levels (magic force) while performing specific rituals or spells. Now comes the fun part; let us learn how to create our magical items.

CREATING A STAFF

Who needs this item?

    Wizards
    Druids
    Magi
    Necromancers.

What Do I Need?

    Knife or similar carving utensils
    Long stick (Bamboo would be best)
    Magical decorations
    Adhesive material for attaching decorations

The Steps

Step 1: Pick up a long wooden stick. It must not be flat, but it ought to be at least as tall as you are, ideally higher. Do not single out just any piece of wood. Search, look around. Balance it in your hand. Feel the energy. The 'right' staff will find you. We endorse wandering in woodland by foot (you should take pleasure in walking the earth), and assemble a proper number of thick, tall and strong branches (make sure it does not break easily).

Step 2: Grant it a unique title. It is your magical staff, and it belongs to you; its title should transcribe its magical bond with your powers, sculpt the title upon the staff, make sure to carve the name in the tongue in which you utter spells; we discovered that if you inscribe in Aramaic, your staff will work best with Aramaic Spells and Magic.

Step 3: Get a knife or a equivalent carving item to mold the staff, if it needs fashioning. You may only wish to expose the bark off it, or to keep the knotted wooden look. The style is up to you.

Step 4: Embellish it. Any decoration is up to you, you can have many decorations or none; the choice is yours. Necromancers will use darker ornaments, as Druids will use decorations of nature, Wizards generally use Stones (stones can be very powerful), Magi may use Diamonds (that will be a stretch, but do not use a false diamond), Witches may use natural materials as well.

Step 5: When you are done creating your staff, it is wise to let it gain power for three days under the full moon. Let its energies grow and authorize its link with your Mana. Remember, a Staff is an extension of your magical sovereignties.

Step 6; Soak the staff in holy water (water untouched by humans) you can find them in a remote natural spring.

Necromancers will use the sixth step differently; to maximize the magical forces of your staff, you should leave it in a burial ground for three days and three nights, and spend time meditating there while holding your staff. While you are holding the staff, you should deliver spells and curses of the Harba de-Moshe Book, which will elevate your authority to speak with the dead; try beckoning the demons of Goetia with your new staff, the more you do with it, the more influential it will become.

Magical Decorations Can Include:

Druids should use feathers.

Warlocks can use glitter.

All Shall use nail polish marks (the glowing/luminescent sorts are great for this).

All shall use sequins, or craft-jewels.

Tie a string on the top and attach some lucky beads, or something that may be personally special to you; if you feel called to do so, go ahead and use a strong glue to attach a hawk feather or crystal to the top.

Use nail polish to preserve the wood.

<u>Warning</u>

Do not tear a stick off a live tree. This is ferocity towards nature, particularly if you hope to come to be a druid or a nature-wizard.

From the scripts of Osari The Wise
(section 2, page 12)

"I bear the staff of truths; it was made by me upon my leading year, in my faculty of magic; The staff has my energy, my apparition, and a portion of my soul; none else shall use it, none else shall benefit magic or charm with it, it is selfishly my own." – Osari the Wise, 1907.

Creating A Magic Wand

Many witches use wands to focus their energy when uttering spells and performing rituals. You can purchase your own wand in New Age shops. However, making your own wand is a particular magical experience that will increase the force behind your magic.

Step 1: Walk alone in a solitary forest. Search for unique sticks and branches you can use; it should be about 12 inches.

Step 2: Remove the bark layer with a razor-sharp blade and carve your desired shape. Use scorching to alter the shape.

Step 3: Alter your wand. You can use plumes, gems, runes and herbs to decorate the wand. Furthermore, you can add strings or symbols that are significant to you, and embellish its exterior. Proceed with any design notions that come to mind and change its shape.

Tips

To give your wand a better look, sand lightly and apply Tung oil (natural oil derived from the seed of the Tung tree).

You may wish to bless or consecrate your wand ritually, before using your wand for practicing

A wand is a personal item that is connected to your Mana. Lending or borrowing wands is an idea that often results in less powerful magic.

CREATING A MAGIC RING OF POWER
(Advanced)

This is a highly challenging item to produce; considering that you be obliged to possess a truly enlightened rank to produce a "feeble" magical ring, and to hold a remarkable knowledge of the divine if you wish to manufacture a pure magical ring of power. Note that you should design the ring, and only you can work it.

Molding a magic ring, using fragments and scraps of gold, is something you can do in your own home. By using a few materials that are immediately attainable in the market, you can produce your individual enchanting ring in a day.

Step 1: Sketch the ring by outlining the shape on a piece of paper. For example, you can design a "ring of fire," or an energy-producing ring. You may be required to begin with a simple design at first.

Practice with one or two simple rings before you start adding extra ingredients. At first, you could use a "ready-to-wear" ring cast. However, it is significant that the making is your own, and your mana (energy) and authorities are focused into the rings.

Be sure to proceed after obtaining the preceding steps; if you took the time to study the books mentioned in early chapters, and could invite true enlightenment, this step will succeed.

Step 2: Produce a ring cast based on your sketch. There are many forms of wax molds that you may use to yield your ring mold. You can buy it online.

Step 3: Round up some gold or silver. Take all of your gold and put it into a clay melting pot. If you do not own a crucible, you can use an old clay jar. Make sure it is sufficiently durable to melt your gold in it.

Step 4: Melt your gold with the acetylene torch. The acetylene torch gets hot enough to melt your gold. Be sure to wear defensive goggles and leather gloves when you handle the torch. Gold should melt quickly.

Step 5: Pour the melted gold directly into the ring mold, allow it to cool; while the ring cools, read the spell you created out loud while delivering Source Energy into the ring. This will transfer your magical energies into the ring; you must be in an advanced level to do this.

Step 9: Remove the ring from the mold once it hardens, use the ring exclusively for the use of casting spells and delivering magic.

Seasoned magic ring-crafter can add diamonds and jewelry onto the ring, engrave the title of the ring and its aim onto the gold before it cools; if you are able to carry out a high grade of magic, you can try to craft a ring particularly for that occasion.

From the scripts of Osari The Wise
(section 2, page 12)

"I carry the ring of Berith, as a suggestion to the day I beckoned my command upon him; The ring is made of silver; it aided in possessing him under power; the scrawl on the ring pronounces:

'The authority of God I command, the rules of Berith the diviner, chief of twenty six legions of demons'".

– Osari the Wise, 1907.

The Seeing Eye

This crystal ball will permit you to divulge with spirits and deities (perhaps God himself, if you are authoritative enough), and will also authorize you to visualize the forthcoming and the destiny of others. The practice discovered by Druid conjurors, and was later adopted by occultists, seers, gypsies and individuals fascinated by the past, present or future. Although Palantirs are habitually made from beryl, rock crystal and other clear stones, progressive practitioners are often interested in forming knick knack objects as outfit ornaments, or for exceptional effects. Additionally, commissioning a genuine crystal ball is too expensive; the comprehension of designing a master crystal ball from absolute is recognized only by few. However, this should not mean that you are incapable to produce such an artifact. You must attain a genuine crystal ball (if you choose to buy it); cost varies between $500 or more. If you are in a progressive state, you will convert an ordinary crystal ball into your very own Palantir.

Step 1: Purchase an original crystal ball, a modest one should cost around $500, authentic nature crystal balls can only be found in museums or shops and will probably cost around $5,000+.

Step 2: Climb to a lofty peak of a mountain (walk up the mountain, do not drive). Aim to reach the highest peak possible. Carry the ball with you during the trip to the top.

Step 3: When you reach the mountain top, hold the ball and meditate, focus upon the "conveyance" of magical energy to it.

Step 4: Osari the wise claimed to meditate upon the mountaintop from sunrise to sundown for three days, while taking short breaks for food.

Step 5: Cover the ball with a clean cloth and do not let anyone else touch it.

Step 6: Create a divination spell or ritual and make use of the crystal ball to communicate with the souls and energies of spirits, demons or angels.

You could meditate with it to preserve its powers; when you focus upon it, you will be able to divulge with spirits, angels and daemons. You will be able to see the past and the future; this will become a considerable spring of knowledge for you, a mirror into the divine world.

CREATING A GRIMOIRE

The grimoire is your journal. Your grimoire will contain instructions on how to create objects like talismans and amulets, how to perform magical spells, charms and divination and also how to summon or invoke supernatural entities such as angels, spirits, and demons. Record your experiences, the information you receive from spirits and demons, and the lessons you learn along the way. Be sure to record effective spells, emotional states and mantras.

You can create many other magical items, such as:

- Magic Sword or Knife
- Magic gun
- Magic Cloaks And Cloak of invisibility
- Magic Rods
- Magic Book or Spell-Book
- Magic Gloves Of Magic
- Magic Pipe-Weed
- Magic Stone
- Magical Amulets
- Magical Crown
- Magical Crossbow

And much more...

Forming and Casting Spells

Spells are often uttered, written, or constructed using a distinct set of ingredients. Preparing your own spells can be learned in the Book of Raziel Ha Malachi.

Due to the very nature of Magick, each spell should be highly individualized and distinctive. When following a conventional spell, it should be fashioned to your particular requirements to be most productive for you. Gaining knowledge of the fundamental principles of Spell Construction will grant you the choice to design your own specific, productive spell for any intention you desire.

Preliminary preparation is needed. You should first determine your sought-after result. You should choose the time to compose and practice your spell carefully. You should consider all Astrological implications, energy streams and Moon stages. The Moon has an extensive authority upon us; we should choose a time when the Moon is in an astrological sign which is relevant for your working. The highest energy occurs at the time of Full Moon and, therefore, this is the best time for provoke magical works.

Begin by gathering all the 'tools' you need for the creation of the spell. If correctly created and used, your tools will provoke crude energetic responses. They should be picked with care. Contemplate upon the spell's "objective" and choose your tools accordingly. For example, if you are planning a 'sexual spell', your candles, oils and fragrances should bring forth a sexual energetic feedback. If the desired result is tranquility, then the tools should make you feel peaceful. The candles used should be applicable for your working.

Prior to your ritual, clean and purify your tools. This is where the magical meditation can become useful. Following a meditation, one should use candle flame, fragrant herbs, bath salts or sensuous oils. Special precautions and appropriate lighting, combined, can produce the tranquil sense required to clear your mind of all earthly thoughts. Your ritual should set the particular energy vibrations beneficial to your aim. You should utilize the mana generated during your magical meditation to provoke a result.

Do not spread your focus by aiming to cast more than one spell. Remember that magic is the manipulation of energy, which is transmitted into the physical world by brain-wave vibrations. A "thought" is a form of energy and visualization is the "tool" with which you broadcast that energy into the physical world. Your visualization is the tool by which you command the magical energy you are producing. You must "know" what you want; you must clearly see it in your mind; you must "feel" the high-energy sensation and direct it towards your aim.

One of the most important elements in the practice of any form of Magick is the Universal Law of Cause and Effect. This means that whatever you do (or don't do) you cause something to happen.

Love Spells

Many think of love spells as a way of forcing someone else to find them sexually irresistible. In fact, love spells should be 'unrestricted' and this form should be utterly selfless. To try to influence the mind of another person may well go against the principles of many wizards, though such spells do tend to be too conventional for many practitioners.

Anyone who desires to cast love-spells should be mindful that such spells are considered "bidding-charms" and therefore should be used carefully. Love spells are generally shepherded by contributions or gifts, which are also meant to affect the recipient.

Bidding Spells

Commanding someone to do something against their free will, evidently demands a great deal of authority and energy and could misfire, causing the spell-caster a good deal of difficulty. Therefore, it is wise to pursue bidding spells which will only be in harmony with the greater good –so no one should be harmed in any way. The practitioner must choose their words cautiously.

Blessings

These require a passionate focus upon delivering peace of mind or healing to the recipient. They hold no threat or risk for the practitioner but are more demanding to acknowledge since they tend to be more inclusive than other forms of magical work. It is the primary focus of pure and positive thoughts on behalf of the practitioner towards another human being or beast.

Healing Charms

Within this form of spell you will ask for healing on all levels of existence – physical, energetic, mental and spiritual – because the wizard may not have the comprehension to authorize him to analyze a "weakness" accurately. Your mana, natural energies and brain-wave vibrations are heightened by invocations, incantations and blessings when combined with visualization. In the "physical" world, material objects such as stones and crystals are 'supercharged' with mana and magical energy to absorb and focus healing or other energies in a particular way. This energy can affect the physical body and aid it in the process of self-healing.

Incantations

This form of utter speech increases the wizard's level of awareness. It set out to call upon the powers and attract the desired level of energy (mana) needed to perform a specific task. Incantation is most effective when spoken with great passion and combined with visualization. An incantation is a productive way of magnifying consciousness and affecting our physiology.

POTIONS

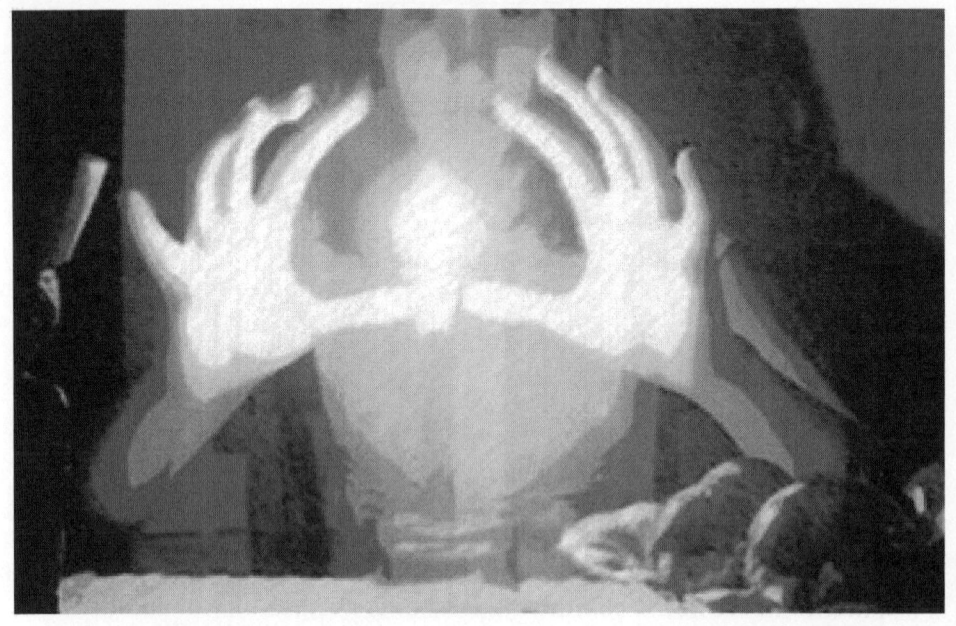

The potion is a concoction, crafted by the wizard or witch for the purpose of attaining a magical purpose. It could be used to heal, bewitch or poison people. For example, love potions make a person fall in love or become deeply infatuated with another.

Potion-crafting is a practice of alchemy and is considered the best-known form of magical practice, a ritualistic formula designed to bring about a particular effect. You must understand the magical qualities of each plant, herb and flower. You use these plants and utilize their energies to create the potions.

Here are a few examples:

Acicia - Protection, Psychic Powers
Adam & Eve Roots - Love, Happiness.
Adders Tongue - Healing
African Violet - Spirituality, Protection
Agaric - Fertility
Agrimony - Sleep
Ague Root - Protection
Alfalfa - Prosperity, Anti-hunger, Money

Allspice - Money, Luck, Healing
Almond - Money, Prosperity, Wisdom
Aloe - Protection, Luck
Aloes, Wood - Love, Spirituality
Althea - Protection, Psychic Powers
Alyssum - Protection, Moderating Anger
Amaranth - Healing, Protection, Invisibility
Anemone - Health, Protection, Healing
Angelica - Exorcism, Protection, Healing, Visions
Apple - Love, Healing, Garden Magic, Immortality
Apricot - Love
Arabic Gum - Purify negativity and evil
Arbutus - Exorcism, Protection
Asafoetida - Exorcism, Purification, Protection
Ash - Protection, Prosperity, Sea Rituals, Health
Aspen - Eloquence, Anti-Theft
Aster - Love
Avens - Exorcism, Purification, Love
Avocado - Love, Lust, Beauty
Bachelor's Buttons - Love
Balm, Lemon - Love, Success, Healing
Balm of Gilead - Love, Manifestations, Protection, Healing
Bamboo - Protection, Luck, Hex-Breaking, Wishes
Banana - Fertility, Potency, Prosperity
Banyan - Luck
Barley - Love, Healing, Protection
Basil - Love, Exorcism, Wealth, Flying, Protection
Bay - Protection, Psychic Powers, Healing, Purification, Strength
Bean - Protection, Exorcism, Wart Charming, Reconciliations, Potency, Love
Bedstraw/Fragrant - Love
Beech - Wishes
Beet - love
Belladonna - astral projection *DEADLY POISON!!
Benzoin - Purification, Prosperity
Bergamot, Orange - Money
Be-Still - Luck
Betony/wood - Protection, Purification, Love

CLXXXVII

Once prepared, the ingredient should be combined with speech to achieve your magical purposes, such as in forming a potion for love, hate, success, failure, protection, purification, and more. You can purchase any of the countless brands of herbs and plants at botanicas and occult shops, and you can create your own by employing the distinct energy characteristics of each shrub or herb. During the process of creating the potion, use a combination that either communicates your particular aims, or is sacred to a particular force planet, deity, element, sign, etc.

Final Words

Good wishes on making it thus far. It is our candid intent to encourage you when reading this book. Whether you prefer to exercise white magic, dark magic or both, we hope you do so in remembrance of the true nature of magic: God.

To grow into an un-imaginary influential wizard, you need to read as much as you can. A true wizard devotes 60% of his or her time reading, and we advise you to do the same. We are working on releasing the scripts of Osari the Wise, which, for some reason, remained mysterious and were never published.

Knowledge is what makes a sorcerer do what he does. He operates outside of the agreed conventions of society. For knowledge, he proceeds into mental places that even the finest men would run from. Always remember that comprehension and intelligence is power. Knowledge holds the cosmos together. Knowledge gives the wizard aim in a doubtful world. When you are low spirited and the skepticism of the physical world upsets you, remember that the command of magic can give your life purpose.

Wizardry is best used by those who are academic minded. However, the walk down that supernatural path will be difficult. At the same time, that is true for almost everything. The saying, "What would you do if you had the power?" takes on a very individual and consequential significant when applied to Magic.

LIST OF BOOKS TO READ

- Holy Books of Thelema
- The Book of the Law
- The Great God Pan
- The Book of the Dead
- Tibetan Book of the Dead
- The Sworn Book of Honorius
- The Greater Key of Solomon
- The Lesser key of Solomon
- The Kabala
- The Book of Revelation
- The Book of Thoth
- The Gaia Hypothesis
- The Book of to bit
- The Torah (Jewish Bible)
- The Bible (Christian Bible)
- Harba de-Moshe
- Sefer ha-Razim
- The Zohar
- The book of Moses
- The Tree Of Life
- The Book of Daniel
- Lesser Key of the Goetia
- Book of Ceremonial Magic
- Hermetic and Rosicrucian Mystery - AE Waite
- Meaning of Alchemy – AE Waite
- Ordo Roseae Rubeae et Aureae Crucis – AE Waite
- Pictorial Symbols of Alchemy – AE Waite
- Some Deeper Aspects of Masonic Symbolism – AE Waite
- The Doctrine and Literature of the Kabalah – AE Waite
- The Hermetic Museum – AE Waite
- Book of Satyrs
- The Focus Of Life - By Austin Osman Sare
- The Complete Golden Dawn
- The Necronomicon
- Devils and Evil Spirits of Babylonia
- Witch, Warlock and Magician
- Principles Of Psychic Philosophy
- Spiritualism and necromancy

- The Canon - Magic Symbols, Ancient Rituals & Divine Magic
- The Book Of Knowledge
- Book of Breathings
- Book of Going Forth
- Witchcraft Today,
- The Book of Abramelin
- Holy books of the Hindus
- Atharva Veda
- Book of Occasional Services
- The Vision and the Voice
- Book of Conjurations
- Grimoires
- Book of Enoch
- Julius Caesar's Commentarii de Bello Gallico
- Book of Taliesin
- Tomer Devorah (Palm Tree of Deborah)
- Book of Genesis
- Island Possessed
- The Book of Lies
- Ordo Templi Orientis
- Book of Shadows
- The Meaning of Witchcraft
- Sefer ha-Razim
- The Malleus Maleficarum
- Book of Virgil's
- Book of Raziel the Angel
- Book of Secrets
- Sefer Adam
- Century of spells
- Introduction to magic
- Ancient Christian magic
- Magic shield
- Grimoire Of Armadel
- Book of black magic
- Book of sacred magic of Abramelin the mage
- Magick, Book 4, Parts I - IV -Revised
- Techniques of high magic
- Compedium Of Herbal Magick
- John Dee's Five Books Of Mystery
- Black Pullet

- Karanina's Book of Spells
- 21 Spells of Domesius
- Ancient Conjurations and Invocations
- Potent Protection Spells
- Book of Shadows
- Practical Candleburning Rituals
- Charms, Spells, and Formulas
- Spell Crafts: Creating Magical Objects
- Complete Book Of Spells, Ceremonies & Magic
- The Good Spell Book
- Book of Spells, The
- Tarot Spells
- Wizard's Spell Compendium, Vol. 1
- Moon Magick: Myth & Magic, Crafts & Recipes
- Spells for the Solitary Witch
- Crone's Book Of Charms & Spells
- Everyday Tarot Magic: Meditation & Spells
- The Salem Witches Book of Love Spells
- Book of Ballymote
- Books of Daniel and Ezra
- The Golden Builders
- Book of Loagaeth
- Liber Loagaeth
- Book of Remembrance
- Spiritual Enlightenment
- Book of Deuteronomy
- Book of Mark
- The Necromicon
- The Book of Abramelin
- Book of Exodus
- Book of the Sacred Magic of Abramelin the Mage

Your Story Continues...

WWW.HOW-TO-BECOME-A-WIZARD.COM

*   *   *   *

Visit the site for daily news, articles, videos, and much more

CXCIV

Printed in Great Britain
by Amazon.co.uk, Ltd.,
Marston Gate.